The Lipstick Ends of Tomboy Femmes

The Lipstick Ends of Tomboy Femmes

by
Annika Geraldine Sparkles

To Astrae, Maelada and Milo

Introduction

This book is not a typical book in the sense that it has an explicit plot or a narrative. It is not a memoir either, in that the original sources of text were never intended to be autobiographical. This book is rather a collection of shards of time lifted from the internet representing a desperate and necessary journey across a shattered patchwork of media, art, myths, experiences, relationships, notable events, love, loss, reverie and pain. These passages enumerate, but do not explicitly describe the experience of a trans woman attempting to find an occulted sense of self in everyday life; attempting to put together a picture of identity where no clear story can be told or recorded. This collection is an epistemological manifestation of self-evident truth.

The contents of this book come from 6 different social media accounts all belonging to myself. 3 Facebook accounts, 2 Metafilter accounts and one Tumblr account. The passages are intermingled and presented chronologically. I have not indicated which shard comes from which account, but I have preserved the timestamps as I lifted the passages, which are thankfully all different. In this manner you may be able to ascertain which passage came from which site.

The legend for determining site source is as follows:

Monday, May 1, 2013 at 1:37pm CST facebook.com
2013-1-05 1:37:16.159   metafilter.com
1 May 2013   tumblr.com

A quick word on editorial license: These comments were lifted from a specific context of time and place. Broken loose some of these comments provide little insight to the moment at hand, but yield other insights that I felt were important to provide. In these instances I have edited many of these comments to provide keys and clues to help re-establish context.

In other instances of editorial license, I have changed the wording and made revisions to the comments in order to account for biases, assumptions and ignorance that I held at the time the comment was made. The most extreme instances of this type of editorial revision are where I made statements that are rooted in unexamined biological essentialism. I have attempted to remove this wording as surgically as possible in order to preserve the intent of the comments.

For the studious among us, many of these comments are publicly searchable. If you would like to see those comments in their original form you may search them out and dive into the threads to gain a deeper understanding of the mise en scène that created this praxis of post-internet occulted identities searching for an implied reflection of self in the broken mirror of existence.

Annika Sparkles,
October 28th 2016, at 10:30.43 AM CST

2014-01-14 22:34:58.783

Dysk,AoK,Yeoz,rtha,Hoyland,Jiawen,Nowtherearetwo, Betafae
and many more helped me find my way.

And Corinth. Damn. I forgot Corinth. Sigh.

Cascadia

Monday, January 21, 2013 at 1:37pm CST
Everything begins again. Moving off this square and onto a new one...

2013-2-28 9:58:16.159
I've known since I was five that I am a girl inside a boy's body, that I was different from the other boys. Years later, after a lifetime of physical, verbal and emotional abuse, depression, failed relationships, self-loathing and self- medication, I have come to accept that my body is, well, female. It makes not a damn bit of sense but that's what it is.

Here I am 33 years later, and I still feel that central truth I knew at 5.

A six-year child can most assuredly understand what is wrong, as I did at that age too. I hope children can someday live in an age where people understand being a trans girl and support it, rather than whisper about the child being girly and gay while they let the schoolyard bullies try to beat it out of her (me).

Transgender is real. Accept it. Kids know it and under-stand it better than anyone, because what they feel is so natural and unencumbered, then they smack head on into a reality that expects them to be something completely opposite what they are. I grew up transgender in an ig-norant environment and it totally fucked me up. I'm in therapy now coming to terms with it. I wish when I was that age I had the support and love Coy Mathis has today.

2013-05-11 01:47:53.833
I don't even know how to approach shopping yet. I went to the Gap and hyperventilated. Walking past Forever 21 and American Apparel explodes a sparkle tsunami of delicious excitement with a nauseating undertow of debilitating anxiety.

2013-05-20 12:37:25.717

When thinking of gender dysphoria (male and female) imagine the problem as software written for the wrong machine that affects a person at a physical level and despite all efforts to "fix it" with thoughts and presentation, the physical issues (anxiety, depression, confusion, inauthentic social life, failed relationships, alcoholism blah blah, the list goes on) never seem to go away.

Currently, the best understood method of solving this issue seems to be to change your hormonal makeup to that which matches the software in your head and do your best with the rest (sexual reassignment, mastectomy, breast enhancement, facial surgery, facial hair removal, etc). It's not perfect, but it helps.

Talking about trans issues now tends to fall back on binary models, but the binary model will not hold up to scrutiny over the long term.

There are intersections in all of this, finding those intersections is the important work.

2013-05-24 22:31:51.407

I think we are all best served if people consider each transgender person a unique individual with a personal story unto themselves and consider each story on a case by case basis.

I believe that if we try to limit generalizations, broad insinuations and over-prescriptive pontification we can have a meaningful dialogue on this topic about the fears and concerns people may have in a way that limits the accidental marginalization of people going through this. Just my two cents.

2013-06-17 22:40:57.073
Joni Mitchell is etched into my heart so deep.

When I was 19 I was deeply in love, lost in San Francis-
co, staying in youth hostels, riding my bike all over that
goddamn city. Court and Spark was on a mix tape, given to
me by my best friend before I left, who I was I madly in
love with and was the reason I bailed on Dallas. I left
on a cross-country Amtrak journey to SF in an attempt to
run away and nurse a love that could never see the light
of day, me a punk shit, her the beautiful daughter of a GM
exec.

Every facet of Court and Spark is a love letter carved into
my psyche. The whole thing. It was my life at that time. I
conquered the hills of SF listening to that album on a Sony
Walkman. I must have listened to it a thousand times over
the two months that I listlessly roamed that city, with
*sour grapes because I lost my heart...a troubled child,
breaking like the waves on Malibu*

Tuesday, June 18, 2013 at 1:03am CDT
Tracing the back road varicose veins of my heart's map, as
narrated by Joni Mitchell.

2013-07-21 14:24:33.593
I see Libertarianism as a tidy, yet flawed ideological
framework that relies on people buying into too few core
ideas while simultaneously ignoring whole swaths of cul-
tural experience that inform and influence actions. This
limitation is what makes the whole ideological framework
ridicule worthy in my mind.

It's too reductive, hell, seductive to actually be useful.
The thought that is missing from a libertarian's thought
process is that "all these laws and ways of doing exist
for a reason, and I should probably assume those reasons
are ultimately just"

The libertarian belief system is pinned to this arc of US
history: The formation of the first federal bank, recon-
struction, the formation of the federal reserve and insti-
tution of the UCC, and the passing of the civil rights act
by the political powers that be eroded individual freedom
and liberty, paving the way for a global dictatorship to
emerge. The core belief is all those historical actions

were inherently wrong and unjust, that they went against what the founding fathers wanted for this nation.

The problem is that the libertarian ideology only reads one side of the arguments presented in the federalist papers, then acts like those pesky opposing viewpoints either don't matter or don't exist. When all views in the federalist papers are accurately represented in a framework, libertarianism as a philosophy cannot rationally exist.

The founding of this nation and formation over time is an astoundingly complex system of conflicting beliefs coming together in a glorious mess, you can't just pick out a handful of historical actions then try to warp them into your viewpoint, instead your viewpoint needs to be informed by the context under which those decisions were made at the time, and any counter factual claims to the contrary are just inherently wrong to make.

When libertarians talk about the civil war or the civil rights act, they are being at best over-privileged and casually racist. It's inherent in the belief system, you can't pull the casual racism out of libertarianism and pretend it isn't there, because without that casual racism it's no longer libertarianism.

I have concluded that libertarianism is an arbitrarily right, reactively hostile, overly reductive framework that cannot be rationally discussed because in order to believe in it one has to ignore the actual historical record in favor of dismissive hand waving when something doesn't line up. It's a tidy viewpoint that simply does not, and will not ever work in a large post-millennial society.

I was a Texas libertarian for ten years, I believe I know what I'm talking about. I voted for Andre Marrou in 1992 if you need to test my cred.

2013-08-24 08:01:13.443
Part of the trans experience can include trying to "fix it" by various means, and those means typically create more misery.

2013-09-01 10:40:48.25
The trick of depression is that it is a lie, the depression wants to exist, so the thought patterns are developed to reinforce it.

Someone once gave me the advice to "flag that thought" every time I went into self-loathing mode. Once I realized the bad thoughts were all lies that the depression was using to build a wall around itself, I was able to dissociate from the depression and look at it objectively from the outside, as opposed to looking at myself from inside the depression.

The depression is warping your thoughts, it wants to exist, it's using your brain processes like a parasite to create an environment where it can thrive.

Flag the bad thoughts, they aren't true. Starve the depression of its fuel.

2013-09-06 13:48:18.42
I don't know jack shit about Yahoo.com, but I do know that artists and designers exist for a reason and that engineer types need to learn the lesson that math doesn't solve all problems equally.

That new Yahoo.com logo is milquetoast crap, it looks like an engineer CEO led a committee to design it one weekend on a lark.

2013-09-07 08:58:01.18
If the majority pointing and laughing at the minority is the worst thing that happens to a marginalized group trying to noisily organize and get their message out, then I'd consider that an improvement over most cases, which usually involves tear gas, arrest, jail time, prison and murder by cop.

2013-09-19 19:31:35.82
I used to live in Deep Ellum in Dallas in the mid-90's and I hung out with homeless people all the time. Most of them lead really messed up lives, but I'll be damned every time

I was short a little money to get a slice of Pizza I could always count on my homeless friends to give me a buck or two to make up the difference.

Ask me about the time we smoked a joint in front of a cop while we talked to him about his day.

2013-09-09 04:40:23.91
I'd like to enter a new word to our lexicon:

Ponfighticating.

Fighty, incessant pontification that only serves to grind someone down to the point they give up trying to reason with you.

2013-09-30 09:17:33.773
People are amazed I grew up in Texas. They say "But you sound so smart!"

2 October 2013
Something As Simple As Mascara

Some days I'm holding on by a thread, a single image, a weak gravity well holding my body to these X,Y coordinates. For several weeks now this has been a memory of standing in the bathroom, having drunk myself tipsy enough to find the inner courage to uncap the mascara and feather out my eyelashes, staring in the mirror and slipping into euphoria, forgetting what it feels like to be "boy" and seeing myself for the first time as "me", fully aware, wide awake, in love with the gift of life. Trans. Feeling a calm wash over me like a warm tingling hug, wide-eyed giggling in gender-liminal reverie. Standing in the bathroom, finally proud of who I am becoming, wondering when I will have the confidence to walk around the block as myself.

Months later, light years away from that bathroom in Tacoma, in what has become the most difficult situation of my life, I have never been further away from my truth. How do I even do this, becoming what I am? I could spill out a million words explaining my situation, desires, wants, ideas and plans but not a single word would amount to any meaningful action that would propel me towards the image of myself in my mind.

The fears are immense, anxiety flits upon my will as I paddle along the event horizon of inward collapse.

How to surf these waves. How.

4 October 2013
Hiding in the doorway

I basically have a queer family. My uncle is a cross-dresser, my aunt is in a Boston Marriage, my cousin is a mostly transitioned FTM and I'm a totally in the closet MTF. My mom is completely cishet and my grandmother thinks the whole damn thing is funny.

So why the hell am I scared to come out? Well, first off I'm middle-age, have a career and a wife and kids and I fall under the "but what about your life?" concern-trolling transphobic line of questioning. That and being a repressed MTF lends itself to all kinds of life instabilities that according to everyone else can be corrected if I'd only just "be the rock" and "the strength of the family" and "the father" and oh my god fucking shoot me if I have to hear that one more time. I can't deal with this, I'm not a man. I'm not a man. I can't be your man. short, my life is a huge fucking mess and on the one hand, why add transitioning on top of it, but on the other, not transitioning guarantees more of the same mess.

So, here I am in the middle, wanting to take matters into my own hands and dealing with a maelstrom that I have helped create out of my own ignorance.
Every day I slip more and more back into the repressed life. Tectonic plates are grinding and something has to give

2013-10-07 15:37:25.733
The weed is too damn high

12 October 2013
Tippy Toed in Girl Mode

"You have to remember to breathe"

"Okay"

"And stop looking away from me to see yourself in the visor mirror, you'll have to look at me if I'm going to be able to put eyeliner on you"

"Okay, I'm sorry, I'm just trying to watch what you're doing so I can learn"

"Just look at me okay, there will be plenty of time to learn how to do this yourself, but right now we need to hurry if we are going to see the set. Now look up."

She brought her lash curlers to my eyelids. The Shiseido eyelash curlers we bought in Seattle this summer at Uwajimaya on a cool summer day, one of those cloudy summer mornings before the clouds burn off and the afternoon blaze sets in, on the day we went to Jefferson park and watched our son play in the water park, where we took pictures of the Olympic Mountains and the Space Needle and selfies. Those days we were looking to the future, unsure, but hopeful, before the real trials began to set in, before we understood the worst was yet to come.

On the day we scored the Shiseido curlers we found just enough reason to feel like we won the day's battle, a ration of faith slightly enough to carry on, enough to weather the remaining days' bumps, if the bumps would only stay small enough.

As we sat in the 4-Runner this hot October night in Austin, in the halogen glow of the street lights, she squeezed the curlers. I felt the sweet pinch and pull on my lashes. In my chest an anxious excitement rose like an ancient aquifer rising to the surface. I felt dizzy and weak, like I was about to pass out. My entire body tingled.

I took deep breaths until I was treading my emotions, bobbing on the waves of panic and desire. Approaching liminality, I hung my soul in her heart, her commands - my instructions, lost in her will, dissolute in my euphoria.

2013-10-18 09:16:23.83
Whoever this "universal woman" is, I'd like to meet her someday!

Friday, October 18, 2013 at 5:32pm CDT
Mae is tying Milo to a tree. Me: (to self) "I'm glad she's working it out, whatever it is..."

2013-10-29 12:06:19.273
So, I'm Popeye the Sailor Ma'am? Or am I Sailor Moon?

2013-10-29 02:20:38.683
In my opinion the binary representation of gender as the predominant gender model creates all kinds of problems for people trying to understand how they fit into the world. Two quick examples, but by no means exhaustive or even representative might be, say, a cis lesbian saying to me "but you aren't a girl" (and if she doesn't like my body type, I can live with that...) to say, a bisexual pangender person who might love being glamorous, fab and femme, but really wants to interact in the world as a man, not a sex object.

We need better language models for this stuff. I think if we were all better tuned to the cues, we could easily see this in people and respond appropriately. I think most of us, however, (even some transgender people!) are stuck at an almost preschool aged level of gender understanding. Searching for an analogy, it seems like it could be an emotional intelligence type thing.

I know myself, I'm a fairly run of the mill trans story that falls into a binary spectrum, and with dysphoria added to the mix means that I'm moving to whatever version of "girlmode" works best for me. That does not mean the gender binary model is most correct, in reality it causes huge issues for me, many unresolvable under the current regime.

If we as a species can get into that nuance and form a deeper understanding of gender, then articles can be written in such a way as to not accidentally cut out people for whom gender divides in the current model with indivisible remainders.

2013-11-02 12:15:37.29
Passing for me is all kinds of distressing. Mainly because I don't at all.

Sunday, November 17, 2013 at 9:07pm CST
"...And I can't keep lyin' all the time..." I have an unhealthy love for mid-90's Magnetic Fields.

2013-11-20 22:39:56.02

I feel so many things and don't really know how to express it. I read the stories about trans people committing suicide, being murdered, losing jobs and facing discrimination all throughout the year, I check up on my trans friends, worry about them, feel stupid for worrying, wonder how you all will find out if I go jump off a bridge. I know the stats; I worry about how I'm going to deal with finding out something bad has happened to any of my trans friends. I was feeling a little too hopeless and decided that going to the vigil in Austin is too much trouble, kids gotta eat, right, but the reality is I'm still mostly in the closet IRL and getting ready for Transgender Day of Remembrance was not going to happen, and showing up in full boy mode...well... Truth is I'm scared of what I am.

Much love to all my transgender friends here and elsewhere. My heart is with the families and friends of the transgender people who have lost their lives and faced abuse this year. I'm sorry that I was not strong enough to show up in person this evening and show solidarity.

2013-11-24 18:29:06.507

Ween is of a specific early-to-late 90's vintage with an exquisitely disturbing and trashy bouquet up front, followed by a long finish of superbly placed intellectual piss, vinegar and fox's ass. Unfortunately the lot's decanting life has well passed its optimal date, but cases kept cool and out of sunlight can still be found and are best enjoyed at raucous moments of unkempt nostalgia.

Wednesday, December 4, 2013 at 9:35pm CST
1. The universe is really complicated and large.
2. I'm an ignorant fool who knows diddly squat.
- The two most important lessons I've learned in life.

2013-12-29 07:26:13.867

The big idea I believe matters here is that Fallon Fox is literally fighting to be recognized as equal to her class. She is up there not to be good, or bad, but to fight, to be allowed to try to win, just like any other woman.

We can scarcely hand her that dignity without first examining her hip size under a hypercritical microscope.

2014-01-10 22:26:15.117
Maybe it would be helpful to point out that I am trans and
I have to face my own internalized transphobic behavior
all the time. It's a thing that happens. Maybe if we could
be less defensive when being called out on acting in a
transphobic way it would help. We're all going to do something that is transphobic at some point or another, what
really gets old are the same typical defensive reactions
and counterarguments in response. Transphobia is actually
kinda funny to me, like pointing out someone has a booger
on their face. It happens, big deal, let's face the issues
as they come up, get past them and move onto better dis-
cussions.

2014-01-21 10:09:07.843
Golf is like Fashion, selling you pseudo-scientific bullshit in an attempt to make you *feel better* about your game.
Whether that game is on the pretend pro level fairway or
the pretend model runway, the idea is to sell you on the
idea that you got something special in your bag. People are
gonna sell sunshine up your ass all day long to make that
sale and we all play along.

If she's a con, then everyone who sells you an oversized
putter or "100% more pretty microbeads" face cream is a
con as well.

In this respect V was not a fraud. She was doing the same
damn thing every other golf huckster does. IMO, her being outed as trans is the lynchpin of the con angle in the
story, and to me that just sucks.

Tuesday, January 28, 2014 at 6:02pm CST
If you want to understand my worldview you must first know
I was raised on Bad Religion

6 February 2014
Shoulders.
And how to live with them.

16 February 2014
Silenced
All my words are stuck inside me, it's a big mess, but at
the end of the day no matter what I do to explain being
trans to the people closest to me, everything gets fucked
up, I'm a boy to everyone close to me, they are telling

me I'm a boy and that I need to accept that I'm a boy and be happy that I'm a boy, even though the truth is that I have been and I'll always be a trans girl. Given the level of total shit I'm catching from people I've decided that I might as well pass as a boy and give up trying to live out as a trans woman. Sorry trans sisters. I'm not strong enough to do this, I feel like I am betraying my tribe, but my life is totally falling apart due to me starting to come out and I have to stop this process before I lose total control of everything in my life.

I'll leave this blog post up for anyone who cares, but I'm fairly certain that I'm done with all this.

Back to my regularly scheduled repressed life…

24 February 2014
Bargaining
Okay, so I'm a girl, but like, I pretend to be a boy, do the boy thing but really I'M A GIRL and being a girl is my secret identity, see, because, amiright? That's okay right? I can fight for justice for trans women wearing this boy mask…and…really…no…? It's not some cute head canon, I'm not a heroine, I'm a traitor. how do I?

Friday, February 28, 2014 at 9:11pm CST
The internet is a perpetual reminder that everything I have ever thought might be apt and clever has not only been already pondered, but has been perfected, polished and discussed to the point that it renders my perception of myself as clever into a fine-ground glassy dust googled right back into my face.

12 March 2014
Ma'am
I've given up transitioning, yet today I was called ma'am at a pizza place while standing in line. The gentleman quickly looked away upon realizing that I wasn't a gender queer FTM, so I seized the moment, smiled and said "It's okay, I prefer being called ma'am".

13 March 2014

Tsunami

Dysphoria suppressed is quietly lapping at the shores of my conscious mind. Arriving as twinges of anticipation, embarrassment, desire and fear when I run my hand across the camisole on the top shelf of the closet or when I watch my wife putting on that cute forest green AA tunic and tights. I sense the tsunami. The swells are near. I will be washed out to sea, to freedom.

1 April 2014
I put my face under a laser for the first time.
It hurt. It felt wonderful.

Things are happening.

Saturday, April 5, 2014 at 1:52am CDT
Transgrrl

Transgrrrl Riot Babe

Saturday, April 5, 2014 at 3:04am CDT
Annika Morgan changed her profile picture.

Monday, April 7, 2014 at 8:29pm CDT
If you want to understand me, google "Understanding Mechanisms of Gender Dysphoria and Its Treatment"

13 April 2014
Facial hair is falling out
I can actually look in the mirror for the first time in my life and not feel ashamed at what I see.

Tuesday, April 15, 2014 at 3:25pm CDT
I'll be appearing on a pre-recorded segment on KOOP radio Wednesday April 16th at noon central time using music as a launch point for a conversation on stepping into the world as a trans woman. Topics include coming out, being trans, married and raising a family, transgender 101 topics and transgender care. The playlist includes music from Vena Cava, The Lovemakers, Unrest, Magnetic Fields and more.

18 April 2014
I came out to HR at work today
They were fantastic.

20 April 2014
I want to be attractive and striking
I see pictures of all these beautiful trans women and fear all I'll ever be able to muster is a monster in a dress. I have the right to be an ugly old woman, but damn that's the last thing I want.

21 April 2014
I don't think our marriage
Is going to survive gender confirmation.

27 April 2014
I moved out a week ago
I'm at the house this weekend with our kids and my heart is
breaking. I can't say I'm blameless, I'm not a victim, but
I've spent my 4 decades on this earth lonelier than I ever
realized. Coming out and trying to live my gender identity
is putting a spotlight on just how deeply these wounds cut.

6 May 2014
The beginning of week 3
Of living on couches and in spare rooms and any other tem-
porary spaces I can figure out. I'm trying to keep my com-
posure. I'm afraid I'm slowly losing my ability to do so.

Hey everyone, I really appreciate your support, kindness and understanding these past few months that I have been fumbling my way "out". I have not clearly communicated how to address me so I totally get if you feel awkward when running into me IRL. So here's how I feel about all that name and pronoun stuff:

1. You can call me Greg, or Gregory and I'm fine with that. It's totally still appropriate right now as I'm not anywhere near being able to present even a half-assed looking girlmode yet.

2. You can call me Annika or Anni for short when you see me and it feels right. If I look ridiculous please tell me, I'm still at 11 years old when it comes to gender presentation.

3. I don't really like being called bro, but I'm not going to get all bent out of shape about it.

4. Calling me girl/girlfriend totally rocks my world. Very soon more things will begin in earnest to start taking care of the biochemical side of my body. Over time my body and face will change in appearance. As I go through this process there will come a time that all the various aspects of my gender will line up better and I will be present in the world more naturally in my girlmode, as opposed to my gender presentation right now which is "failing at trying to look androgynous". As I go through this process please do not worry about offending me or anything like that and if you have any questions please ask, I'll do my best to answer them. I know this is awkward and different, and again, I really appreciate how awesome everyone has been about this. Much Love, Anni

26 May 2014
If everything goes according to plan I'll start HRT 5 days
from now.

29 May 2014
The doctor's appointment is Monday at 10:45, here's to
hoping for a filled prescription.

3 June 2014
HRT Day 1
So I guess June 2nd is now a special day :-)

Sunday, June 8, 2014 at 5:02pm CDT

I started hormone replacement therapy (HRT) a week ago. HRT for trans women, for those who don't know, is the medical process of lowering Testosterone levels and raising Estrogen levels in the body. You can google it, wikipedia has a pretty good page on how it all works. One week in and I am already noticing subtle internal changes are occurring. The most noticeable is gaining a better ability to filter out the continual "thought storm" in my head. I've already seen this ability help me drill into priorities/issues at work and more effectively drive them to completion. The next most noticeable things are, internal resistance to getting started on tasks has lessened, my anxiety levels are a bit lower and I feel like more of the world is getting through to my senses - that I am able/allowed to be more present and participate in this world as "me". Emphatically, HRT is the best thing I have ever done for my mental and physical health. For the first time in 40 years on this planet I feel like I have the right to participate in "being human". Getting here has not been an easy journey. It took me over a year to get access to this treatment and I have had to overcome major roadblocks and significant life changes to get to this point. For me and thousands of other trans people, gender dysphoria has a medical solution, it's not a "choice", we are not doing this to be on a stage or for attention. The biggest reason I feel compelled to share this with you all is the hope that by sharing my experiences I can help people understand that access to transgender care is an imperative option for trans people, that it is time to end the social stigma and remove the roadblocks to adequate treatment. Love you all.

Monday, June 9, 2014 at 4:24am CDT

I was a fool, but I am now the stronger fool, can we suppose that counts for something in the marathon of sharing out your heart?

12 June 2014

HRT, Day 11

Woke up at 3:45 AM, took a bath and cried more. I cried for being able to love myself, for finally wanting this body and wanting to take care of it, I cried or finally feeling love again after 10 years of darkness, I cried for never being able to be the man everyone expected me to be and not being strong enough to know how to say "I am transgender" years ago before I took on the challenge of being a man and hurting my family as I fell apart. I cried for the pain of 4 decades of not being able to fit in and feeling awkward and embarrassed for being a girl. I cried for loneliness, I cried for our kids, I cried for Angela, I cried for our love, I cried for my heart to heal and spill out and wash over the world and give all of myself to love, out of honor and respect to have been given the gift of this trans woman body and the chance to be alive again to live my remaining days in MY woman-ness. I felt humiliated, naked, in the tub with my dysphoria, my awkward body, probing, touching, sensing, wondering, waiting.

I got out of the bath and played guitar for a while, I cried for our music equipment scattered in disarray and disuse. I cried for my guitar not having sung my songs for the past year, I cried for the neck of my guitar not feeling my grip and I cried for the nape of my waist not feeling the cutout of the guitar as I held her snug to my body and sang and played and tears fell onto the strings and into my lap and I played and sang again after a year of no music in my heart and cried for all these things.

Thursday, June 19, 2014 at 8:01pm CDT
#FirstWorldTransGrrrlProblems: I need to wear boyshort underwear with the style pants I wear (stretch, mid-rise, regular cut) and I cannot for the life of me figure out which part of my waist to measure to get the sizing right...you can't just...try them on to see...I mean...gawd.

Friday, June 20, 2014 at 5:22am CDT
Insomnia is creative lust pulling back the shadowed curtains.

Monday, June 23, 2014 at 1:05am CDT
I love you all, even those of very few of you who are totally pissed off, hurt and angry at me for seeking hormone treatment for my gender dysphoria.

2014-06-25 15:40:41.57
I wish I could quit this country.

Thursday, July 3, 2014 at 10:27pm CDT
Tonight I sent this text to a friend in need, and thought
someone else might need it also: "...you have to also bathe
yourself in your hurt, figure out what caused it, those
painful memories you don't want to look at, those things
you did you regret, the dreams you fucked up because you
were too afraid to pursue them, the women that broke your
heart, and what you did to make them leave, you gotta look
at that regret and heartbreak, that hurt, that dream you
had as a kid and failed to impress, you gotta look at that
kid inside you and say "I'm sorry, I fucked up, but I love
you and I'm going to keep fucking up for a while, but I ha-
ven't forgotten about you and you are worth fighting for".
And fight for that dream you had as a kid."

2014-07-04 09:14:28.87
Taking my son to the fireworks stand on the Indian reser-
vation down at the Port of Tacoma is one of our favorite
memories.

Sunday, July 6, 2014 at 6:22pm CDT
I was so down low and numb for so many years and coming
back to the surface is bringing me up through stratified
emotional layers of disappointment, anger, grief and anxiety. The process of fixing what's broken requires owning
those feelings with resolute fury and compassion, being
totally real with everyone around me and surfing a wave of
simultaneous collapse and in-place creation. This isn't
fun, and it isn't pretty, I know it may be worrisome, but
it is not bad, nor is it the end of the world.

2014-07-08 15:39:54.033
I think my feelings and thoughts crystallized this morning
as I was riding my bike to work, from the home of yet another person I've met who is being generous enough to let
me sleep in their home for a few nights while I get myself
lifted off the streets, with everything I can possibly
carry in my backpack, trying to figure out if I have enough
money on my target gift card to buy toothpaste, realizing
that I am almost out of all my toiletries and how am I
going to make it to payday with only 22.50 remaining without starving and smelling, all because I started Hormone
Replacement Therapy and my soon-to-be-ex-wife asked me to
leave the house and I obliged her request because staying
there causes terrible fights and I cannot take the abuse
anymore, and the kids sure don't need to see that. But re-

member, I left, I abandoned my family because I chose to seek access to medical care to deal with being born transgender. It was my choice, right? I mean, I'm "choosing to be a woman" and I am just dealing with the consequences of that "decision I made to stop being a man". It's bullshit, but this is really how it is to try to live as an out trans woman.

Is it too much to ask to just show some fucking compassion and abandon careless adjectives that harm people you hardly can be arsed to give a crap about? I mean, what does it cost you really? Because I am paying a pretty hefty goddamn price right now for being a trans woman that very few else of you here willing to help cover, and thank goddesses for the few people who have reached out and helped me through some pretty seriously fucked up circumstances these past couple of months. Against this milieu of my current trans narrative, I'm saying, that no, really, it would be nice for people to stop using the word "tranny". It literally harms no one to give that word up (and hell of a lot of other ones as well).

2014-07-10 12:48:50.207
I was trained how to be a boy though merciless bullying and physical and verbal abuse starting in 4th grade that lasted all the way until 8th grade. Any privilege that was extended was held in exchange that I not show or reveal any desire to express myself as woman. This was not a covert or subliminal message, it was very direct and made plainly clear to me.

After the physical abuse stopped because the boys realized how terrible it was, the verbal and social reinforcement continued, well, even to this morning, as I am not fully out yet at work but I am also not giving a damn anymore about hiding my womanhood.

Male privilege extended to a trans woman is a "gift" held in exchange for hiding your true identity, and I am constantly reminded how tentative that privilege is being extended based on how men gender police me daily via subtle comments and taunts. This shit is real people, and claims that I am somehow tainted by that privilege, and that somehow due to that taint I harm cisgender women, are really fucking awful to my ears and trigger hard-to-curb suicidal feelings.

2014-07-13 14:40:03.45

Trans women are women. period. Include us in your defini-
tion. That means some of want to be female, and we have
medical options to pursue in order to be female, end of
story. We aren't a threat and we don't create any situation
that denies any other woman access to care. Science makes
available to trans women options to be female in every
meaningful way that matters in everyday functional life,
society and civilization.

As women, the options available to us to be scientifical-
ly designated as "female enough for everyday reasons" are
routinely denied. Like how women with a working uterus are
denied birth control or access to other forms of afford-
able and preventative women's care. The care I require as
a woman does not match fully 1:1 what other women may require, but it's still women's care.

Past a certain point of HRT and other surgeries, "science"
can call me female and not give a fuck, while future ar-
cheologists would designate me male due to the effects of
testosterone on my skeletal structure, but that really
doesn't mean much of anything to me right now and shouldn't
to anyone else in everyday conversation either.

Thursday, July 24, 2014 at 10:47am CDT

So, here's an important update, everyone: Since my last
update on "Pronouns and What to Call Me", a lot has changed
in my body and presentation and I move through the world
as a woman now. Therefore, my name is Annika, I am a "She"
and "Her". Please use that from now on, thanks!

(I won't be pissed if you make a mistake in real life,
but on facebook you have a backspace key, if you get it
wrong, use that functionality please) Also, Jon Esteve is
the only person on earth who gets to call me Ms. Assface
Bossypants.

29 July 2014

Update: I have a place to live after 3 months of living where ever I could find a friendly couch, I've been on HRT for 8 weeks and life is awesome. This has been the hardest time of my life, yet everything has gotten so massively better on the other side of this hardship.

Friday, August 1, 2014 at 10:03am CDT

Today is the first day "officially" in my new place. Little things feel a bit surreal still, like, having my own bathroom for instance, or having an empty bedroom and realizing all I have is a bike and a bag to put in it. But it is my space and I am grateful. I have spent three months living on couches, cots and people's generosity and here I am, almost exactly one year to the day of arriving back in Austin after a still bittersweet goodbye to Tacoma, having closed one book of my life and looking at the empty pages of another waiting to be written before me. Here's the list of awesome people who have all showed love and support through what has been an extraordinarily trying time, my heart aches under the weight of the love I hold for each of you: Leah Velleman and Cait, Libby Wong, Ulf Kastner, Beverly Towb Ridley, Margret Pearce, Melanie Towb, Natalie Ridley Baerwaldt, Maelada Echo Coneflower, Astrae Lucia Coneflower, Milo, sweet little milo, Mad Elaine, RK Ghostley, Nathan Klayman, Somer Leigh Suter, Joshua Browning, Liz Larsen, Rachel Kronkor, Mitch O Kronkor, Erica Shelgren, April Dawne, Danaca Tomas, Montana Piñeyro, Joleen Jernigan, Kate Davis, Alicia D. Hartzell...and many others... Much, much, love to you all.

2014-09-08 10:43:56.903

As far as transphobia goes, yes, trans people internalize transphobia. I do, I face it and try to deal with it every day.

Sunday, August 10, 2014 at 2:21pm CDT

I carry in my heart an ember of bright happiness underpinned by unimaginable frustrations at the way certain aspects of my family life have played out. Going into details would not help anyone, but suffice to say I carry a mix of disappointment and anger lurking under the surface that in private moments, consumes me.

Tuesday, August 12, 2014 at 5:38pm CDT
Yeah so a first of having two construction workers catcall me with a "what's up baby?" and a "You alright?" just happened. I'm feeling half concerned, half validated. #transgirlproblems.

Wednesday, August 13, 2014 at 9:15am CDT
I lead a pretty damn charmed life, people. It's not easy, but it's not bad either. I'm not going to claim I found this river of delightful energy on my own, truth is I've met a lot of amazing people who trustingly shared their secret maps along the way, and for that I am grateful. You know who you are, shouts out and high fives for believing in me through my worst, even those who decided they can't be here with me on my path today. I love you all.

Friday, August 15, 2014 at 5:36pm CDT
Today my HR reps and I met with my manager to inform him that I intend to transition to Annika at work on August 25th. He was fantastic about it. Over the next week I'll be informing my peers and vendors of the change, and Monday the 25th I'll be at work as Annika and everywhere in the world as me. It only took 35 years after I named myself Annika to fully actualize it, the world feels a tad brighter this afternoon. (Be the person you promised yourself you would be when you were 5 years old! I'm living proof it is possible!)

18 August 2014
Coming out at work
I'll be going to work august 25th as my preferred gender, name and pronouns.

Good times.

22 August 2014
God dammit
Feeling like I'll always be a "man" in the worlds eyes and that a womanhood shared and accepted by my surrounding community is impossible. Fuck. This. /me takes more estrogen, stares off into the distant hills.

Saturday, August 23, 2014 at 11:16am CDT
Yesterday was the last time I'll ever leave the house using my given name.

Tuesday, August 26, 2014 at 4:34pm CDT
Okay cool. Gender neutral bathrooms at the airport take some of the anxiety away, the TSA agent using correct gender pronouns helped a lot too, but no lie traveling as a fresh-off-the-wrong-gender trans woman is some real deal shit. Stop staring, people, I may be a cute translady but I need to shave and I look like a wreck, lol.

Wednesday, September 3, 2014 at 2:14pm CDT
Gender liminality is freaking weird.

3 September 2014
My god. It's full of stars.
The dysphoria I feel at the gender event horizon on HRT makes the dysphoria I felt a year ago seem absolutely pleasant in comparison. I feel every physically masculine trait with the heat of a thousand stars across the time dilated stretch of a supermassive black hole. Into liminality I am thrust, everything has become unstuck, undone, ambiguous and unsure. Shields up.

2014-09-12 10:44:48.837
I'd like to win an intimate hug in a car that doesn't end
with "we make better friends than lovers"

Tuesday, September 9, 2014 at 7:27pm CDT

When someone talks about a "natural order" to things as a way to express their confusion with me being transgender, I realize what they are really talking about is a "moral order". So by questioning my existence as a "natural woman" what they are actually questioning is whether or not I am a "moral woman". To which I must confess, I am most certainly not...

22 September 2014

I kinda fucked my life up pretty badly on the whole. I mean I did the "right things" but I feel like I wasted my life trying to fix permanently broken situations. And now the rush of life has passed and I'm at the peak looking back feeling like, fuck, I squandered it on dumb bullshit.

3 October 2014

No end. Only pain. I have to live with it. I used to pray as a child that I would wake up a girl. Now I pray that I don't wake at all. I fucking hate this some days. How to live with this?

3 October 2014

I can do it. Some nights are just really hard. Love to my trans women sisters.

2014-10-15 18:06:29.643

Sex assignment at birth is a prison sentence for a trans woman.

20 October 2014

Fuck my body
For real this thing can go die. Now.

23 October 2014

A text feed littered with texts to your ex-wife, canceled dates and being stood up no-shows.

"Welcome to trans womanhood!"

Saturday, October 25, 2014 at 11:44am CDT

I'm sitting here eating tacos with milo, listening to this sweet child tell me how his grandmother talks to him and says all kinds of transphobic crap about me. Stuff like "his name is (insert dead name)" "deep down he knows he's a man" and if he tries to counter with her she gets angry with him and raises her voice and tries to tell him what a terrible human being I am for transitioning. To make it even worse, she goes on transphobic rants about all trans people *to him*. Like what? Why is this milo's responsibility to bear? Why in the hell does a grown woman think that's okay to do that to a ten-year old child? I know the answer and the fact is she does that because she can. Anyway, I'm glad I've only got three people in my life out of the literally thousands I know that think I'm some kind of freak, or have had a problem with me. To those people, double fucking middle fingers. I'm here, I'm Annika, deal with it. (And for epilogue, milo knows what's up and knows his grandmother is wrong. I'm a damn good parent and I raised him to be right and strong.)

7 November 2014

I had through work what was/is commonly called an EAP (employee assistance plan) I called them and said I was having a personal life crisis and I needed counseling. They gave me three free sessions then they were ten dollars a session after. I went to therapy for 3 months and then asked for the letter to start HRT. 2 months before I actually got my letter I booked my first appointment with an endocrinologist in my area for a month prior to getting me letter. I went to my first appointment and they took blood for lab work and I signed all the "you will grow boobs and your penis will stop working" docs. I scheduled it all out so that by the time I went for my "you can start now here's your RX" appointment a month later, I had my letter in hand to give to my endo. That said, I didn't start for another year. Because dumb reasons and live and heartbreak and transphobia and stigma and fear.

June 5th 2013 I had the Rx for HRT waiting for me in Seattle. I delayed it a bit because of work and marriage struggles. I made the decision in June 2013 to move to Austin Texas. I spent that year fighting with my wife, trying to get into a doctor to get my HRT prescription filled, but she was not agreeing to it and making my choice to start HRT INCREDIBLY DIFFICULT. That went from Jun 2013 to April 2104.

In April of 2014 I was drinking way too much. I'd pretty much given up transition at this point. My wife was spending several nights a week away from the house, I know now she was starting another relationship with a guy we mutually know. So one night I'm really drunk and I snap. I went to the bathroom and put makeup on. Dregs of makeup, old stuff that was years old. I didn't care. Then I put on a dress and leggings. I was seriously wasted at this point and got on my bike and rode to downtown in girl mode. I took a picture of myself at rio Rita (cool bar) hung out for a while then rode back home. When I got back home I changed my Facebook profile pic to the one of my girlmode with the caption "transgrrrl" and changed my name to my chosen name, Annika. (My gender was already "she") Then passed out. My wife never came home that night.

I woke up the next day to my family freaking out, blowing my phone up and Facebook messaging me. My wife was a total wreck. She called from wherever she stayed the night furious, embarrassed and crying. This went on nonstop for two days, old coworkers calling, friends reaching out and people either criticizing me or loving. It was out of control.

15 November 2014
If anyone's looking for me
I'll be over here getting constantly misgendered everywhere I go.

Sunday, November 16, 2014 at 10:54am CST
So I'm up at cherrywood right now, buying breakfast tacos for myself and milo...And I leave my bank card at the
counter, without realizing it. This place is packed. A few
minutes later I hear an employee saying really loudly "is
there a (insert legal name) here, (legal name repeated)!".
Omfg. Tripping. I motion to the guy "that's me", he gives
my card to me and I'm just like, welp. Uhh. Hey everyone!
It's not a huge thing but I just wanted to share the little things that happen every day that most people never
experience. There are people up here (employees and cus-
tomers) who only know me as Annika, and now they have that
additional reference point, a reminder that "hey, there's
something different going on with this person". Legal name
changes, they serve a purpose, and this is a reminder for
me to get it done asap...

Sunday, November 16, 2014 at 10:16pm CST
Last night My roommate and I were talking about deep stuff
like we tend to do, and I started talking about the extent
of space to which a person's actual "body" exists within.
We convince ourselves to believe that our bodies end at
our skin, but really, our bodies also extend outside of us,
in the form of legal documents, legacies, intimate spaces
between two people, and also inside each other in the form
of memories, feelings, love, and spiritual connections. I
concluded that our actual bodies exist inside of us AND
outside of us and that what exists of our bodies outside
our skin is largely beyond our control. Therefore, it is
important for all of us to find opportunities to care for
our external bodies as much as we care for the ones that
reside within our skin. I explained how every day I leave
the house I am trying to care for and advocate for recognition and control over my externalized trans body. What my
body is referred to as. For people to allow me status as a
woman. To create a space for my identity and external body
to exist as a woman in the hearts and minds of others. This
is something I deal with every day and was highlighted this
morning at Cherrywood Coffee with the dissonance between
my trans-feminine appearance and my masculine birth name.
When I posted about this interaction to Facebook I was as-
tounded to see other people ALSO advocating for my external
body, by offering to help fund my name change. My friends
came together with an idea and Nathan Klayman created a
BEAUTIFUL go fund me page. I cannot begin to explain how
wonderful his words are at capturing what this feels like.

I could not have written that myself even though I live it. What you all have taught me today is that our external bodies live partly in each other's hearts, and that through the love and support we show for each other, all of us can care for each other's external presence in the world. For my community of friends to come together in four hours and completely fund my legal name change is breathtaking and shows me a world where my physical body is loved, and my external body is given care, recognition and legal status. This has been a bit of magic today, everyone who made this possible, you are all incredible human beings. Much love to you all: Williams Craig Annie Downing Emily Osborn Gena Senibaldi Melynda Prue Corinne Green Brooke Kelty Julie Gillis Lenny Tropiano Carolyn Cunningham Seth List Lisa O. (who are you?) Fox Sircy (and who are you?) Amber Alexander-Zuniga Martha Carol Cone Lauren Manes Jayme Ramsay and Lauren Wroe Kurzman...and one Anonymous donor. You all, for real, thank you so much.

Monday, November 17, 2014 at 4:53pm CST
The certified and signed seal on my court orders. Your love, support and belief in me made this possible. Thank you.

Tuesday, November 25, 2014 at 10:42pm CST

If anyone's looking for me, let them know I'm the gay looking weirdo dude in the back of the bar with blue hair.

Friday, November 28, 2014 at 12:49pm CST

Angela, the kids and I drove into Dallas at the crest of midnight, cleaving Monday into Tuesday listening to the Beach House "Bloom" album. As albums sometimes go, it represents a particularly painful time in my life, the things that I did to hurt Angela, and ways that I untied our bonds through the time period she and I shared the album in our relationship. The minor scales and euphoric swells of the album line the contours of my memories, giving them a soundtrack to rest upon and replay themselves in the back of my mind, taking me to places and times long-forgotten, to feelings resting quietly, waiting to be surfaced and savored, understood and placed, into better context within the storm of our narrative. As we rounded out of Oak Cliff, Reunion Tower rose, her light patterns swirling, a modern lighthouse guiding us into the city. We approached downtown and within me swells rose to surf, surf rose to whitecaps, whitecaps crashed into a single large rogue wave, and my tenuous ballast capsized between the surface tension of the present moment and the inky darkness of unseen memories, as I sank into the deep, the undertow pulled me back to last Thanksgiving at our house in Austin. The tension of a year flexed through body, memories erupted through me and rippled through my mind. Flittering, tattered images of a beautiful thanksgiving day scrolled past. The day, sepia and warm. The house filled with the smell of rosemary and sage. The table prepared with roasted vegetables, wonderful salads, vegan gravy, casseroles, cranberry and homemade pies. In our hands we shared coconut eggnog blasted with spiced rum and whiskey, made for each other, laughing at how strong we made them. We poured good wine for our friends. We danced to vinyl records. We shared all this with our friends and family as the waning sun drifted into the night, we shared all this from love, with those we love, and as the stars rose with the moon, that day soon would become, unbeknownst to me at the time, one of the last days our family was all together sharing a home-cooked meal in deep, intimate smiles, and love and appreciation for each other. The past year has been hard. Transition and divorce is not easy. We have been sad, angry, and in our darkest moments filled with destructive rage. We've shared terrible moments together since that night, but that time does not define who are, or what we are becoming. Since those dark days that became us, we have found a tacit peace with each other, an acceptance, a different kind of love. There is a distance now that in the space between us, I ache endlessly for what could have become, but I appreciate where we are now. I spent thanksgiving this year with my biological family, shared with my three children. This is the most time my kids and I have spent together since last April. The four of us spent this time rediscovering each other, remembering that as a family, though we are unconventional, we are loved, and that love helps us stay strong. I made the same roasted vegetable dish this year that I made last year, the familiar smell of rosemary and sage filled my mother's home. Again there was too-strong coconut eggnog, again there was love, again there was warmth. Astrae played guitar and Mae played violin, they sang to my family and my heart opened. There, drowning at the bottom of this ocean of these memories, sitting at the hot crack in the seafloor of my heart, a love as hot as lava flowed out from within me, made new surfaces, and new memories attached to those surfaces. Our sparse traditions we keep, held across the turmoil, form an unbreakable bond attaching us to each other as we pull apart and grow into our own. It is for that I am ever grateful.

Much Love, Annika G. Morgan

Sunday, November 30, 2014 at 9:12am CST
Came home from an awesome week in Dallas to my new SS card with my legal name. Achievement unlocked!

Tuesday, December 2, 2014 at 10:20pm CST
This is kind of a watershed moment tonight. Most people probably don't know that until tonight I've not slept in a bed regularly since last April, and for the past 4 months I've been sleeping on an REI camping mat and sleeping bag on a floor in a largely empty room. I'm finally "home". Refusing and putting away survival mode and trading it in for thriving mode. In the words of Operation Ivy: "to resist despair is to resist everything." Thanks Niki Nash for helping me move in and set up tonight.

Thursday, December 4, 2014 at 12:45pm CST
The dissonance between "I like where all this physical change is going!" and "Are strangers in the ladies' room freaked out by my physical appearance?" makes for a strange reality to navigate some days...

Friday, December 5, 2014 at 5:07pm CST
Disney's The Little Mermaid is a pretty damn good trans allegory.

Monday, December 8, 2014 at 11:32am CST
The lipstick ends of tomboy femmes.

Eerie Goddess

2014-12-08 12:37:37.787
From my experience, even though I grew up in a totally gen-der-neutral environment WRT to "what girls and boys do and how they are allowed to play", it's really important for parents in the community to be inclusive of trans children when discussing the inevitable discussion about what body parts do, why they exist and what they mean. That time of my life is where the "girls" separated from the "boys" in a very serious way, it was the trauma and othering began in earnest, and marked the earliest stages of repressing myself and suffering in silence. This was at about 7,8 years old.

It's not easy for parents to grasp the notion that "sex parts != gender" and even harder still to put that into language for children. Yet it is a big deal.

2014-12-18 07:17:00.527
Being trans is innate for me and I don't have to prove it to you.

Friday, December 19, 2014 at 8:08pm CST
Listening to my son tell me how people around him refer to me as "it". Then he starts in on a trans right's rant about how my "...name is Anni not it". Kid has my back, that's for certain.

Tuesday, December 30, 2014 at 11:08pm CST
2014, what a hell of a year this turned out to be...a year of darkness, brightness, roughness, deep cuts, physi-cal damage, shapeshifting change, gender transition, name change, separation, love, no love, lost love, found love, grudge love, emergence, depression, great friends, sup-port, tons of love and support, hope, followed plans, achieved goals, new looks, discarded attitudes, discovered attitudes, better ethics, remorse, reward, and now, here at the year's end, a shiny new awesome project is lined up on the runway ready for takeoff. 2015 is shaping up to look awesome. Thanks everyone for all your love and sup-port this year. I am still here, thriving over surviving because all of you showed me that I belong in the world as me, that I can stop being afraid of my truth. Love.

Friday, January 2, 2015 at 12:54pm CS
When the cashier at the coffeeshop asks "What changed about you, something is different" and all I can think is "scientific sorcery, love".

Saturday, January 3, 2015 at 9:38am CS
On New Year's Eve my bandmate Niki Nash delivered the smack down to someone who helpfully pointed out to me "So, you're a tranny?". Last night Justin Sweatt, one of my favorite artists in Austin (Xander Harris, Red Ox), gave me the best "you got this, I got your back, keep kicking ass" talks since coming out and starting transition. Hugest of hugs and rays of light for these two amazing people who inspire me to be my best and give me hope to power through every day undeterred.

Monday, January 12, 2015 at 9:18am CS
Pondering imaginary interview situations... Interviewer: "...describe your biggest weakness" Me: "I'm really, really, white..."

Saturday, January 17, 2015 at 12:19pm CST
2015 goal: get a car. Being a twee trans girl on the bus is too nerve-wracking.

Thursday, January 29, 2015 at 9:03am CST
One of the best things I've come to understand is that good feeling I had when I would wear my mom's clothes to school under my boy clothes in 4th and 5th grade is how most people feel when they wear what they like on the outside and that the feeling I had is not bad or otherwise something to be ashamed of, it's the good feeling that comes with being yourself. Hopefully that offers a little insight to you all the little ways people can be confused at fundamental levels for decades. Anyway, that's all I gotta say about that.

Thursday, January 29, 2015 at 8:33pm CST
Still, to this day, when a movie gets to a sex scene I have to make some stupid remark like "they're gonna do it!" You think I'd have grown past that by now. But alas.

Sunday, February 15, 2015 at 5:22pm CST
Apparently gender queer parenting leads to questions from Milo such as "which one of Adam and Eve was the boy?"

Friday, February 20, 2015 at 12:51pm CST
People ridicule a masculine body in feminine dress. People celebrate a feminine body in masculine dress. For two months now I have been moving more to a feminine gender appearance and the amount of harassment I receive in public has gone from "doesn't happen" to "happens multiple times daily". It has been suggested to me that my feminine style of dress is causing my problems and that I would move better though the world in a more tomboy-femme appearance. It has also been said to me that feminine clothing itself is oppressive and all women would be better off avoiding femme dress in most settings. So, if I want to wear what I want to wear, then I feel certain camps of feminists feel like I am throwing the efforts of second-wave feminism in the faces of all women. Meanwhile the public at large outside a few people treat me like I am an offensive joke. Transfeminine womanhood is either living in conflict or avoiding conflict. Every day for me lies this decision: Where to reduce the conflict by dressing tomboy femme, or increase the conflict by dressing more twee/light femme. This situation is pissing me off greatly. I feel like my unwanted male puberty has been a prison sentence that I'll never be able to fully escape because so many people think a transfemme apperance is gross and/or offensive and it makes them uncomfortable, and I am in the position of having regulate other people's disgust and discomfort by how I choose to present myself every day.

23 February 2015
Dysphoria days are like:
(Look in mirror, try to take a selfie) Go to hell, my body. Fuck you, my face. Except you, my little trans lady boobies, you're okay, we're fine together. (Cups breasts, looks down) MY HANDS!!!omfg…

Tuesday, February 24, 2015 at 10:46am CST
This bill will fail, but the overton window is so far on the side of hate in this legislature that I fear I will be 70 years old before we see actual, real support for quality of life and access to care for trans people residing in this state.

Wednesday, February 25, 2015 at 10:36am CST
Your body is at the core, pure possibility, continually working to achieve a more complete expression of selfhood. That is the basis of what "is" is, and nothing else besides

you can define what and who you are, and are becoming. To deny someone that possibility is to perpetrate violence against them.

27 February 2015

A majority of the weirdness all in my head is from being in a liminal gender state and trying to figure out where and how I am allowed to claim my gender and live in social spaces without freaking out. The reality is clear though, most people really don't care. They really don't, and the ones that do don't matter. I have to take anti-anxiety meds to deal with my internal anxiety as a I go through this and the clarity I gain from taking meds is instrumental in being able to think clearly and claim spaces with relative ease. I know it is hard, I know there is passing privilege and all kinds of dynamics that can harangue and beleaguer trans women, but the goal here is to claim space for your-self, and I know you can do it. Hugs, love and light, the struggle is real.

Monday, March 2, 2015 at 8:11pm CST

It's hard being a ladyboss. But no mistake, I am your la-dyboss.

Friday, March 6, 2015 at 5:33pm CST

Accidental work skype chat poetry:
we can take a break from this
let's pick back up monday.
We are deep in the witching hour
and beer is needed

Wednesday, March 11, 2015 at 9:25am CDT
I am a transfemme earth scout for the supergoddess of love
and destruction.

Sunday, March 15, 2015 at 3:57am CDT
Me: downtown
Her: walks up
Her: "what's your name?"
Me: "Annika"
Her: "no, I mean your real name"
Me: "Annika"
Her: "no, I mean the name you really go by"
Me: "Annika"
Her: "no, I mean the name that is the name you actually are"
Me: "Annika"

It was funny in the moment. I hate it now.

Monday, March 16, 2015 at 2:29pm CDT
Apparently I look like a dude today. I can't force my gender, I am whatever my body decides to throw out there on any given day. Sometimes my gender mode is stable, other times it is not. I am learning how to better move with this fluidity of my biology. it does not affect my sense of self as cute woman, so it's not like I have an internal problem with myself at all. What I do have a difficult time with is being treated differently when my "boy-ness" projects. I feel uncomfortable and alien. It's a construct in the world I can vaguely recall, and one I am glad I am able, at times, to escape. But alas gravity has pulled my gender presentation to planet boymode for a minute, and I remain firmly affixed to my trans woman vessel, looking out, putting it all together. Strange times indeed.

16 March 2015

There's no right path. I took 18 months and three tries before I finally locked into it and told myself that this was going to happen no matter what the consequences. Almost a year later, after losing my family, being homeless for 5 months, getting divorced and struggling with my internal crap I can say that it is slowly getting better. It's hard. Really hard, we all have things going for us and things fighting against us and some of us start out with more resources than others, but for as difficult as this is, honesty, willingness, the ability to gracefully move past mistakes and celebrate wins, while finding good friends who will let you lose your shit without judging you while you figure this mess out will be instrumental to you finding the light and love inside yourself that you know is there. You can do this, I promise.

Thursday, March 19, 2015 at 8:22am CDT

When getting ready in the morning I think things like "in a post-apocalyptic dystopian future, q-tips won't exist." Then subsequently feel a renewed determination to ensure that our civilization can continue to thrive.

Monday, March 23, 2015 at 6:54pm CDT

Back to long stressful days at the Datacenter, but this time carrying fond memories of: dancing to Das Ding, Marie Davidson, S U R V I V E, Flatliner (that Juno 6 arpeggiator!) Boan, Chastity Belt, Jacco Gardner, Tele Novella, Happyness, The Octopus Project, Wray, Ukiah Drag, Elvis Depressedly, Diamond Age, Def Rain; feeling proud of my daughter Astrae Lucia Foneclower; playing a lovely Charm Bracelet show with Niki Nash; and getting my shoegaze on with Rachel Staggs as Experimental Aircraft, and A Tiger Named Lovesick. It was a magical week, bittersweet I descend back to mundane stresses, recharged and renewed.

Thursday, March 26, 2015 at 1:34pm CDT
I'll just be over here. With a cute top on. Backwards.
Shit.

27 March 2015
Don't tell me I'm an attractive Trans woman, show me. Show
me.

Tuesday, March 31, 2015 at 3:01pm CDT
For Transgender Day of Visibility I went to the Texas Cap-
itol with a group of a dozen or so trans identified people
and cis allies to put a name and a face to the word transgender. We broke into teams and each team met with aides
and staffers of several representatives to share how our
lives are impacted by several bills currently in committee. I'm excited to work more with Cavan Ó Raghallaigh
and Equality Texas to stay on top of the legislature to
ensure that everyone who identifies as transgender in the
state of Texas has a chance to live a more fully authentic
life free of hassle and fear. If this sounds like work you
would like to help with you can reach Cavan at: cavanor@
equalitytexas.org and he'll be glad to get you involved in
the process.

Wednesday, April 1, 2015 at 8:49am CDT
After probably...12 thousand listens of Court and Spark
over the past 22 years since I first heard it, I'm going to
have to admit that "raised on robbery" is a totally obnox-
ious song.

Monday, April 6, 2015 at 5:36pm CDT
One day and one year ago I changed my name and profile pic
on Facebook in a totally despondent state of trans-dys-
phoric hell, determined to do this. One more-intense-than-
anyone-can-imagine year later I'm still surfing the uncer-
tain, divining more questions than I could ever answer,
resolutely standing atop the flow.

2 April 2015
Beautiful monster
My sex at birth, orientation, role and presentation are beyond rational comprehension at this point. I've crafted myself into a creation of total confusion, an eerie goddess of dark love haunting this earth and leaving pools of slippery gender everywhere I go, like tar pits poured from pandora's jar slowly gnawing at you and leaving you wanting more of the fear I bring.

2015-04-13 10:49:48.347
In the end you become what you hate if you stay in the technology biz too long.

Saturday, April 25, 2015 at 5:19pm CD
People who throw gum on the ground should be forced to eat that shit.

Transgender Girls, Transgender Pretty

29 April 2015
A Visit to My Childhood Self
Hello? Are you still here?

You're back! I was scared I would never see you again!
I am so sorry sweetie, I was scared too, it feels so good
be back here!

Why was I gone so long?
You were growing up! You skated, played in punk bands, went
to college, started a career, got married, and had children of your own.

Was I ever a pro skater?
No, never a pro skater, but you still skate!

Aw! I wanted to be a pro skater.
I know, life has a way of going in ways we didn't plan for.
Speaking of, I have important news to give you.

What is it?
It's about our secret.

We're not supposed to talk about that.
We can talk about it now, What I came to tell you is that
you tell your secret to the world.

WHAT? people don't kill me?
You stay very much alive! You become the girl on the outside you've always been on the inside.

Does that mean I wear girl clothes OVER my boy clothes now?
You don't wear boy clothes at all now.

I actually wear girl clothes ON THE OUTSIDE?
Yes, baby. You don't hide them under boy clothes anymore.

So I'm a real girl now?
You are a real girl now.

With real boobies not pretend?
With real breasts, not pretend.

How? I prayed and prayed, was told I'm a boy and there's
no such thing as magic!
You found doctors who gave you medicine that helped you

feel better about those body parts that make you feel sad and angry all the time.

The medicine made me a real, actual girl?
You have always been a real, actual girl, a very special type of actual girl, known as a transgender girl.

What's a transgender girl?
For you it's having what people think is a boy's body, when it's actually a girl's body!

But does the medicine make the body parts I hate go away?
Baby, those body parts are still there, they don't go away unless you tell doctors to make them look more like the body parts most other girls have.

But I want to be a real girl.
You are a real girl. You always have been. People said the wrong things to you, they didn't know so much about trans-gender people back then.

Well I don't feel like a real girl. I feel like an ugly pretend girl.
That's called dysphoria, sweetie. You have a really bad case of it.

Dysphoria?
Yes. Dysphoria is something you have, it causes all the sadness and anger you feel about the body parts you were born with.

A transgender girl sounds like…kind of a girl, but not re-ally a girl.
No sweetie, you are a kind of girl, really a girl. A very special kind of girl that's not born very often.

Am I as pretty as the other girls are?
You are pretty in a way that most other girls wish they could be.

Why can't I be pretty like most other girls?
Because you are a transgender girl. And transgender girls are transgender pretty.

Transgender pretty?
Yes. You are a beautiful transgender girl.

Can doctors at least give me the girl parts so I can make babies inside me?
No sweetie, you will never be able to make babies inside you.

But it's 2015! There should be warp speed spaceships and alien contact by now, what do you mean I can't make a baby inside me?
Maybe someday, far in the future, transgender girls will be able to have babies. Your body though, does not make babies. This is something you will have to learn to accept.

But WHY CAN'T I be like other girls!? I DON'T WANT to be a transgender girl. What's pretty if I'm not real?!
That feeling is dysphoria. It never goes away. I promise you though, one April morning in 2015, you will look in the mirror and you will see a real, beautiful transgender girl looking back at you and you will feel the glow of happiness that comes from knowing you are a real girl.

You promise that happens?
Double Pinky Promise.

So..after I feel transgender pretty, do people still make fun of me?
People will always say mean things, but you won't care, you have nice friends who are very kind to you.

What are my friends like?
They are all talented and unique people, like you. They understand who you are and accept you. You love them very much and they love you too.

You aren't going to make me have a boyfriend, now that everyone knows I'm a girl, right?
No, you thought you liked boys for little bit, but you REALLY like girls.

That's good. Don't ever forget how mean the boys were to me.
I'll never forget, love. But I have to say the boys now aren't so bad! There's quite a few nice ones. You should give them more of a chance.

I'll think about it…Do I still have to be called my other

name? I hate that name.
No, your name is Annika now, like you always wanted.

I REMEMBERED MY NAME?
Yes. You told everyone your secret name.

I am so brave!
Yes, love, you are very brave girl.

So what am I gonna do now that I'm a real, pretty transgender girl on the outside?
Well, you work to make the world a nicer place for transgender children like yourself, so they don't have to grow
up in a world where they feel ugly and ashamed like you
once did. You will show the world that trans people are
real people too. That transgender girls can be musicians,
skaters and artists. That we don't have to want to be like
all the other girls. That transgender girls can be any type
of girl we want to be that we are real girls too and we
don't have to keep it a secret anymore.

That sounds nice.
Yes, I thought you would like it.

Can I go with you to do that? I'm scared staying here alone
and you were gone a long time.
Yes, you will be coming along on this journey, but we'll
need to stay close to each other. It's a big world out
there and it's easy to get lost.

Okay. I promise to stay close wherever we go.
As do I, love, as do I.

Team Sparkles

Friday, May 1, 2015 at 2:35pm CDT

May 2015 is going to be one for the record books for me. I don't even wanna go into the details, it's gonna be awesome and I can barely freaking contain myself at the moment.

Thursday, May 7, 2015 at 12:02pm CDT
Last night as I was about to leave Hotel Vegas after the
show a stranger approached me, got 5 inches from my face,
and proceeded to loudly exclaim to me all the things I'll
never be, what I really am and that I'm not fooling anyone. He was a pretty terrible excuse for a decent human,
that's for sure. I don't know the person, they walked off
into the crowd, feeling chuffed I'm sure that he got to
clock a trans woman and call her out. I was alone when
it happened. It scared the hell out of me and I was too
paralyzed to respond. It was a shitty end to a magical
night. His actions don't define who I am or how I feel
about myself. I am glad I have the friends I have who
understand me and accept for who I am. I'm glad he only
told me off and didn't physically assault me, I'm okay,
really, but for a couple of hours afterwards last night I
was in a really bad place. Thanks to the people who re-
sponded to my now-deleted FB post last night and tried to
help. It is very appreciated.

2015-05-09 06:59:10.19
My housemate is getting up and ready to come into the
living room and I'm going to have to tell her that I am
crying about big bird. It's a hell of a lot more than
that, mostly I'm crying for the wonder and amazement and
magic of childhood.

2015-05-11 07:25:21.923
I don't talk about this much, but when I was a *very*
young teenager at 13-14, I was involved with some pretty
terrible skinhead groups. I woke the fuck up and tried to
quit that scene when I started being a part the violence.
I had to seek protection from the Sharps and stop going
to punk shows for about a year. This was about 1988-1989.
The punk subcultures of the 1980's were complicated and
my heart aches thinking about that era and what everyone
went through. I feel it so deeply, the contradictions.
Everything. We're just humans wanting love underneath all
this bullshit and the apparent ideological contradictions
don't negate your desire to seek meeting that need.

Thursday, May 21, 2015 at 11:39am CDT
Dear U.S. Peoples: we'd all sound a good deal sexier if
we said things cost "two pounds eighteh" and what have
you. Just putting that bug in your ear...

Sunday, May 31, 2015 at 5:12am CDT

Niki and I play a matinee Charm Bracelet show at The Lexington this afternoon and this evening the travel duo splits as I'll be heading off to Paris for the week...May 2015 has been a multicolored smear of undifferentiated epic. And you know what, July is shaping up to be just as awesome.

Sunday, May 31, 2015 at 3:35pm CDT

The hangover lounge. Charm Bracelet did it. I'm proud of our little band.

Tuesday, June 2, 2015 at 4:04pm CDT

Today is my one year anniversary of starting Hormone Replacement Therapy. This day is quite possibly the most important anniversary in my life because HRT quite literally saved my life. Being a trans lady is not always fun or easy, but the alternative is worse. I'm a living example of this. This time last year I was in an awful hell of mess. Fast forward one rough-as-hell year later and I'm at the Eiffel Tower, girlfriend of raddest girl I've ever met, promoted at work, traveling Europe and experiencing the most epic month of my life to date. It gets better, I promise, it really does. #translivesmatter hugs and love to everyone who supported me this past year. You all live in my heart and my actions every day. ❤

Post-Caitlyn Transsexuelle

Wednesday, June 3, 2015 at 6:36am CDT
I've been fortunate to have been with limited access to my phone for the past several days. And in a country where no one really gives a shit that I'm a trans lady and calls me Madame and Mademoiselle and the guard checking my bag at the Eiffel Tower sang a song to me in Italian. Caitlyn Jenner, keep on with yer bad self.

2015-06-03 06:56:32.757
I'm one year into HRT as of yesterday and "what the fuck is transgender?" gets harder to explain with every passing day. I think it's best to try not to understand this as something that exists at a point, but is rather a process that needs *a lot* of ambiguous space to unfold.

Just let the gender be in a space for a while, Caitlyn will continue to define who she is, just like we all do and I am happy she's got off to a good start.

Now, personally, I'm not all that "femme" though I do like to "be pretty" every so often. I like having "boyness" but I don't want that to be "what I am" I am girl with some boy in me, not male-centered. I dunno. shit's complicated yo.

Saturday, June 6, 2015 at 3:18pm CDT
Hour 3 of a ridiculously long 36 hour trip home from Paris to London to Atlanta and finally Austin that will involve every form of transit save dirigible. I'm ready to be home. This trip was epic. I feel proud to show Europe that trans women IT engineers and musicians do in fact exist and travel the world. I'll probably write something more prosaic when I'm not hung over on a bus.

Sunday, June 7, 2015 at 6:30pm CDT
31 hours of busses trains and planes. 5 more hours and 1 plane left. I'm beyond tired and jet lagged at this point.

Saturday, June 20, 2015 at 2:16pm CDT
People may not know that I took 18 months in semi-private to sort out in my head exactly what I was going to do before taking any concrete steps to align my identity and body. It was not an easy 18-month period, but it was cru-

cial for ensuring that whatever major steps I took were the correct ones for me. In that 18-month period I prepared myself to give up and lose most of the life I had built up to that point, knowing that everything would have to be renegotiated on terms that allowed me a space to exist. When I finally said "okay I am doing this" I was prepared to lose the comfort I knew and within the span of a single workday I went from "cis" to "statistic".

Homeless, separated, losing my wife and children and tearing down and rebuilding was not easy. The price I and my family initially paid would be more than we could bear without permanent scars and trauma, but sometimes you have to accept one kind of trauma in order to avoid a worse and more severe outcome down the line. Parenting and life is sometimes a real kick in the ass like that.

Despite that, here we are a little over a year after that day my ex and I made the decision that we could not continue together and what she, my children and myself have gained is so much than we ever, ever had before and gets better with each passing day. We all have a deeper respect and admiration growing in the space where before resentment and anger bore toxic fruit. Living authentically is not easy.

If you are thinking about taking steps to align your identity and body, please listen to your own heart before a doctor's words and correctly sort out what's not working and what you are fixing before you ever start.

Aligning and living authentically in your presentation alone will not fix a broken marriage, nor will presentation or HRT re-pattern bad personality traits or undo the damage done by living an inauthentic life. Those things you can only fix by doing the work inside yourself to make yourself a more compassionate person. Those things exist separate from your gender identity, but living authentically can help you over time learn how to become a better person overall.

If there's a point to this rambling, it is to say that if you are considering realigning you gender presentation and identity, I think it's important to know what you are fixing with medicine and changes to your roles and presentation and what *you* need to fix in your mind and heart, then prepare for the outcomes and brace yourself for an extraordinarily difficult process that will test you to the limits of your ability to maintain.

Obergefell

2015-06-26 10:52:20.393
My girlfriend and I just met for coffee and the first thing she said to me was "So, this means you're gonna be my wife someday" and I said "yes it does" and we shared the sweetest kiss I think I've ever had.

Wednesday, July 8, 2015 at 11:05am CDT
Another trans woman has taken her life. Her death hits really close to home and has devastated an online community I am a part of. Her death has broken the hearts of several of my good friends who helped me stay alive through the darkest period of my own life when I wasn't sure I could go on. I don't even know how to process this or bring it up other than to say, please don't kill yourself.

Come, Armageddon

2015-07-15 11:21:39.09
Lord, what have I done?
I have only just begun.
Life seems to work better this way.
Hope you don't mind, I've gone astray.

Thursday, July 16, 2015 at 9:25pm CDT
For reasons (good ones!) I'm listening to Morrissey and
"every day like Sunday" is playing and I'm transported
back to this song playing on a foggy winter Sunday morning,
sitting with Milo at Puget Sound Pizza in Tacoma having
Sunday brunch, feeling every nuance of this song, looking
up at the cashier sharing that "it is known" nod, then all
three of us hollow and overwhelmed, looked blankly out the
window over the translucent blanket of fog covering com-
mencement bay. When the song ended Milo said "I think I
know exactly how he feels, daddy".

Sunday, July 19, 2015 at 11:33pm CDT
<redacted>

2015-08-20 08:25:26.937
To be a creator on the internet for most of us is to surf
the tiny waves on the long tail.

2015-08-26 16:14:39.227
This internet is a community to me. I don't know about you.

I've made friends here. IRL friends that I first met here.

I've met Trans people the world over here, and they all mean a lot to me.

An online stranger sent me money when I was homeless, transitioning and broke with no way to buy medicine or eat, then asked me to pay it forward instead of back.

It's a community, a virtual community where most of us care about being good to each other (even when we get it wrong) and growing into the future, learning, raising awareness, finding the edges of our shared humanity and exploring those edges as best we can with the words we've got.

That means a lot to me. And I hope it does to you as well.

2015-08-27 17:01:11.127
It is harrowing and difficult for trans people to find good, solid, partners who *get it*. Who are friends and lovers and everything and so much more to each other. When that type of love is found, nurtured and developed, the relationship is shared in a way that is so deeply committed and profound, because it's not like there's a bar on every corner where people are looking to seriously date a trans person. You can't just walk away. You have to make it work. You make that commitment and it means you aren't gonna "jump another train" when you get bored or the challenges mount. You stick with it and work through it and do it for the love, because love for trans people *is* rare. It's not something we want to just talk about either, especially when enjoying ice cream and the conversation goes silent and we try to figure out where the conversation goes next. The feeling is known but the conversation doesn't need to go there. Well, Sarah McBride and Andrew Cray had to go there and have that love that is so rare taken by death so soon...

and it cuts to the saddest places inside me.

2015-08-28 08:55:39.23
I was either threatened, blown off, or made to feel ridiculous save for one person who saw me as an actual human worth trying to love, and that person is now my mate. To find her I literally put my life on the line and suffered terrible, shitty circumstances and situations "in the dating scene" to get there. Love for trans people is rare. That matters because a lot of people (in my experience all, save for one) don't believe they could ever see a trans person as a person worthy of being in a relationship with.

I guess what I am trying to say is trans people are worthy of experiencing the same universal love anyone else does.

3 September 2015
Authenticity
Is not "happy" or easy. It's redeeming in many ways, and there's a deep internal joy I feel, but the suffering is just as fucking deep and dark. There are tiny wins. But massive anxieties. Everything has to change. I'm not exactly up to the task of completely rebuilding my life but I have to do it anyway. I feel like a goddamn fraud.

9 September 2015
Newspaper headline: "Is the Crimson Pig dead or alive?"
Porco Rosso "I wish I knew".

This is how I feel about my gender right now.

2015-09-17 18:46:13.04
I remember the sinking panic I felt on 9-11 while holding my 4-month old daughter, looking at the TV as the second tower collapsed. Feeling like it was the end of the world and feeling so bad for bringing my baby into this mess.

Then my grandmother died 1 month later as the bombing in Afghanistan began and I held my 5-month old daughter feeling like the it was end of the world again, worried about the world my daughter would inherit.

Then the 7 more years of Bush drove me absolutely mad.

She's 14 now, doing her homework beside me, a beautiful and bright light, determined to make a difference in the world. I'm betting on her that she will. She's been the one thing that's been holding me together all these years and getting me up and busting my ass every day to give her the best chance she can have. Because she grew up in this mess and still has hope. That means everything in the world to me.

2015-09-22 08:59:35.95
The other day I told my girlfriend that our microscopic skin bugs were probably starting a family together and moving over to each other's bodies to make one big hap-py skin bug family. We both thought that was super cute and wonderfully gross and we kissed each other and talked about how happy our skin bugs will be together, and wished them a long and happy life together.

Because love is freaking great like that.

2015-09-30 07:31:03.79
I don't even wanna think about how crappy a person I used to be, but I was so alas. A lot of life seems to be a continual process of learning how to suck less and feeling really embarrassed at how ignorant we used to be.

2015-10-28 08:12:47.26
People need to realize how minorities bear and carry the social costs that allow the privileged their blithe ignorance.

Thursday, October 29, 2015 at 4:57pm CDT
I really hope Houston passes the HERO ordinance on Tuesday.

2015-10-30 11:46:17.9
You all can miss grantland, but I sure as hell don't

Friday, October 30, 2015 at 3:04pm CDT
Anyone who is sad that Grantland was shut down today,
please remember the time they outed a trans woman and drove
her to suicide before deciding you *really* need to shed
that tear. If that's not enough to suck the tear back in
then please block me from seeing your post. KTHXBYE.

2 November 2015
Approaching Womanhood.
So two years ago I started this blog, after almost of year
of coming to terms with myself as trans.

I'm letting go. I'm a trans woman adrift in the patriarchy. I'm letting my voice come out, my sexuality shine and
my sensuality radiate. I'm here. I'm free from my internal
repression and I'm finally making it out. It's been hard
as hell: isolation, depression, suicidal thoughts, alcohol
abuse, homelessness, periods of no food, getting dumped,
my heart broken, all the while growing into my trans womanhood and carrying this wound inside me and struggling to
heal my pain.

Three years of hell. More to come for sure, but I'm in the
world now, determined to thrive.

Unclipping for now. You got this.

The Coastal Town That They Forgot to Close Down

Wednesday, November 4, 2015 at 7:46am CST
I'm the she-monster in their heads.

Wednesday, November 4, 2015 at 8:51am CST
My thoughts on fucking Houston: I won the trans girl consolation prize of looking cis-pretty enough that I personally don't have to give a single fuck about anyone's translady hard on hate. Cisworld extends to me their 4-day parkhopper badge to Cisneyland because "pretty". Well fuck that I reject it. Women have a right to carry their unwanted male puberty with dignity and without being compared to child molesters. Hugs from an unapologetic and very irritated trans lady.

2015-11-04 10:28:51.87
I seriously can't even with what happened in Houston.
I'm not a predator. I'm not a she-monster. I'm not their bogeyman.

Wednesday, November 4, 2015 at 12:18pm CST
My dad hasn't told anyone at his work I'm trans, because apparently they all think trans women are gross homos or something equally gross like that. They also talk politics and news events, so I imagine my dad is at work today hearing how Houston "showed those queers" or some other bullcrap. And he's probably going along with it. Big middle fingers to the world today.

Friday, November 6, 2015 at 10:25am CST
Hey look, we are all pissed about HERO failing, but supporting boycotts on Houston that seek to remove capital from the city will only eliminate jobs and harm those most disadvantaged, I.E. Trans Women of Color who live in Houston. The answer is not to pull support from the city, but to support the city more.

Wednesday, November 11, 2015 at 7:19am CST
Patriarchy looks like telling trans women it's a bad idea for them to use the women's restroom because men with their uncontrollable jollies will use that to dress up like a

woman in order to gain access to the women's room for ill intent. Does anyone realize how absolutely screwed up that line of thinking is? Let me spell it out for you: TRANS WOMEN DO NOT CARRY THE BURDEN OF MEN - men carry that on their own. Men need to own up to their shit. Denying me access to go pee in order to protect women from poorly behaved and over-privileged men IS RIDICULOUS. If you see someone posting dumb shit to their walls about how gender neutral bathrooms are a bad idea, please speak out in a forceful voice. I'm seriously depending on all of you.

GIRL UP YOU FUCKING MAN TORSO

2015-11-20 14:26:05.033
Due to a couple of massively distressing things that have come to light over the past 24 hours I'm having a really hard time convincing myself that life is worth sticking around for today and the irony is not lost on me that this is happening on Transgender Day of Remembrance.

There are no dots large or dark enough to convey the holes in my heart for every trans person who suffers this world.

2015-11-20 19:13:16.327
Sophia had a tough situation. Her passing was really sad.

Monday, November 23, 2015 at 11:09am CST
If you're a gender critical rad-fem who prefers the abolition of gender or is otherwise angry and pissed off at femininity for existing and think that means you have the right to determine how gender is good or bad for everyone, then please go jump off the nearest cliff. I don't even really give a crap about gender, I'd love for the whole notion of it to go away forever, but don't reduce my struggle with my body to a social construct. That's condescending, belittling and demeaning. Whatever the hell I'm struggling with inside myself lives deeper than pink or blue or whatever hell else gender binary bullshit we were fed growing up. Hugs.

Wednesday, December 2, 2015 at 8:07pm CST
Today is one of those days where I look in the mirror and say to myself "well, the world may have off the rails today but at least I have cute boobs."

Friday, December 4, 2015 at 1:46pm CST
Me at 6:   "can I be in your girl's club?"
Girl at 6: "no, you don't wear barrettes"
Me at 8:   "will I ever wear one of those pads?"
Girl at 8: "no, these are for girl panties only"
Me at 12:   "let's be the bangles for the talent show!"
Boy at 12: "that's so funny! Boys dressed up as girls!"
Girl at 12: "but you actually make a pretty cute girl..."
Me at 15:   "I wish I was a girl"
Girl at 15: "being a girl sucks!"
Me at 20:   "I feel like a lesbian..."
Girl at 20: "all the emo boys say that"
Me at 29:   "I don't know how to raise a boy"
Girl at 29: "it's time for you to finally man up"
Me at 38:   "I think I'm a woman"
Girl at 38: "I think you're a disgrace"
Me at 41:   "I'm a woman now"
Girl at 41: "you didn't have a girlhood, so you can't be"

Wednesday, December 9, 2015 at 7:54pm CST
I took all the misogyny and trans exclusionary feminism
and ableism and xenophobia and racism and all those other
isms from America and reversed that wheel of samsara to
make homemade potato and polenta gnocchi in a "no-chicken"
cream broth. So fuck you, haters.

Friday, December 18, 2015 at 7:41am CST
Super deeply bad body image dysphoria self-harm feelings
this morning. I'm in the middle of this storm trying to
hold on to the center and these are the weeks and months
where I have to remind myself once again: "at least I have
this".

2015-12-17 10:59:46.257
Trans Women gross most of you out. Just admit it and move
on.

2015-12-23 11:49:38.583
Marriage equality without trans protection is not finished.

Tuesday, December 29, 2015 at 4:08pm CST
Remember, it's not you that causes problems on Facebook,
it's your mean ass inconsiderate friends that you keep
around.

Saturday, January 2, 2016 at 9:27am CST

So I've been wearing my black sparkling glitter leggings for three days now and no they aren't coming off today either.

Sunday, January 3, 2016 at 3:28pm CST
2500 dollars' worth of bills in the mail for trans care that is not covered. Fucking fuck.

Thursday, January 7, 2016 at 10:44am CST
So my HR rep can't seem to tell me over email or phone what "options" I have regarding transgender related coverage thorough my employer healthcare. Which would be fine to meet with her but I'm working at the Datacenter all day today tomorrow and Saturday. Feeling like I'm pretty much over it and need to seek employment where trans related care is covered. #inertia

Saturday, January 9, 2016 at 12:44pm CST
I get so annoyed when someone online says to me "I don't believe what you're saying, show me an example that proves what you're saying is true" as if I'm obligated to go into a lengthy back and forth to illuminate strangers on the internet just because.

How about this: Get off your ass and go find an example yourself. I just tell it like I see it and I'm not here to explain stuff to defensive people who don't want to listen and learn and grow.

So, if I say something and you feel defensive and angry and think I'm full of shit and feel like I owe you an answer for what I already know is true, then you can pay me 85 dollars an hour, my current hourly rate, to go google the most basic of shit for you.

Otherwise do it yourself and get the hell out of my face.

Monday, January 11, 2016 at 9:40pm CST
OMFG Estrogen has made my hair absolutely lovely. HOWEVER: Washing it has become a complicated strategy of timing and planning and an extraordinary amount of giving a fuck of where I'm gonna be the in the next three days and if I don't wanna have frizz-ball pom-pom head when I get there. My answer is I just don't wash it much anymore.

Wednesday, January 13, 2016 at 8:11pm CST
I wish I could tell you all the shit I'm dealing with right now, but for all the stories and sharing I do on this damn website there are still some things I don't talk about here. Let's just say I'm taking care of some serious business at the moment and your loving kindness right now is appreciated.

Saturday, January 16, 2016 at 8:58am CST
Holy fuck it just hit me, I don't have cis biology.

So when people with cisgender bodies are talking about how cisgender stuff is not nipples or girl nipples or how babies genetically latch to their bio-mommas or periods or vagina talk this or that or what the fuck the other and I'm sitting there confused and depressed about it because I don't know "what I am" in relation to that it's not because "I'm not really a trans person but just a confused cis person" it really means "my body doesn't have an understood space in the world, and probably won't in my lifetime". But I totally just figured it out. I am trans-bodied.

Regardless of hormones or clothes or pronouns or names or any of that. This body is transgender, and no matter what I choose to do with my body, that this body is a trans body remains fixed and unbroken.

What's broken is the lack of a space for me to rationally and emotionally exist among large swaths of the cis-bodied majority. I'm confusing to you and that made me feel confusing to me but like seriously holy shit I'm not confused at all really.

Sunday, January 17, 2016 at 12:58pm CST
Uterine magic spiritual feminism brings out a lot of really deep self-loathing body crap for me.

"Hey here's a life you'll never get to know, even though every fiber of your being feels robbed that it was never there in the first place. Sorry, less special one, too bad so sad for you."

Monday, January 18, 2016 at 3:04pm CST
Oh jeez I'm on a call and my manager just asked a coworker
to "dig out any nuggets they can find" with regards to some
abusive threat actors targeting our sites. /me goes back
to her mid-90's stoner MTV days and says to self "Heh heh
You said dig out butt nuggets, Beavis"

Tuesday, January 19, 2016 at 3:34pm CST
You know what. Other people can make you feel hopeless and
small. And even if you don't want to give them that power
they find a way to take it from you anyway. I'm sure I've
been that person to others in my not-so-awesome past.

But I can say it is possible for another person to make you
feel like the world is a dark and shitty place, and when
you have someone like that in your life that you struggle
to be free from, well, it sucks really fucking bad and can
make you question the very essence of who you are and if
that's even worth a damn because you're too weak to ever
seem to get away from them.

Tuesday, January 19, 2016 at 5:47pm CST
"well, at least I'm still beautiful." Said I as a I walked
across the parking lot away from my abuser.

Friday, January 22, 2016 at 12:35pm CST
I'm sorry not sorry I made my friends listen to the beauty
and the beast, little mermaid and Aladdin Disney soundtracks
if they wanted to ride in my car my senior year of high
school.

Tuesday, January 26, 2016 at 1:22pm CST
All the feelings are too much and really it's all a pile of
anxiety and regrets right now buried under a feeling like
I wasted the best years of my life on the dumbest bullshit
you can imagine.

Wednesday, January 27, 2016 at 9:51pm CST
When the cashier greets me with ma'am and completes the
transaction with sir. Shouldn't be nothing but a thang but
it is. Sighs. And now I'm waiting in a parking lot for my
eternally late now officially ex-wife.

Sunday, January 31, 2016 at 10:58pm CST
I'm grateful for my friends doing all the hard work making
all the big important good things happen in the world while
I sit here looking at my breasts pondering "if I were to

walk around topless would people assign them female and apply misogyny, or would they assign them male and apply transmisogyny?" I seriously don't know what to think. Like would they be seen as they puffy man boobs or small girl boobs? Weird shit. Y'all keep hashin it out about Bernie and Hillary while I try to figure this out. Hugs and thanks for your continued efforts.

Monday, February 1, 2016 at 8:10pm CST
If I could give anyone the best advice for happiness it would be "learn how to spot a clinically narcissistic person and give them wide berth"

Thursday, February 4, 2016 at 10:54am CST
If being a trans woman doesn't send me to an early grave my ex-wife and the fucking child support division of the state of texas surely will.

Sunday, February 7, 2016 at 6:11pm CST
Me (after long emo spillage of heartfeels) "it's just, sweetie, I feel so heavy, like I'm carrying so much more around on my chest the days." Tina (lovingly) "it's your boobs, they're growing baby"

Monday, February 8, 2016 at 9:29pm CST
Just a few more months of living through the dumbest bull-crap no one should ever have to suffer.

Friday, February 12, 2016 at 5:42pm CST
Regarding the lady who referred to me as "that" when addressing Milo and hour or so ago. I'm having a really difficult time putting that shit away at this moment. I think "maybe she's right who the fuck am I kidding here."

Thursday, February 18, 2016 at 10:40am CST
TFW when you are reading comments where a bunch of cis people are talking about whether or not trans people actually physically exist or should be allowed to. Privilege is the ability to reduce a person down to a thought exercise and giving yourself permission to limit another person's to right exist within your bullshit moral framework.

Friday, February 26, 2016 at 10:49am CST
My coworkers nearby just heard this from me while on the phone with my daughter: "Sweetie, you need to pop your kneecap back into place" #joysofparenting

Monday, February 29, 2016 at 8:27am CST

My current life narrative revolves mostly around "Coming to terms with how my anxiety creates ridiculous barriers to doing the most basic shit."

14 March 2016
When dysphoria divides
It pains me to see a trans person so upset by the "desired looks" of other trans women that she will rage post about how lucky they are and how shitty and terrible she is, then go on to claim that "trans girls prettier than her can't complain". Like what standard to define beauty are we using here that gives any trans woman the right to lord over the good or bad looks of another? She has told me I'm one of those people whose looks cause her severe distress and it's ironic because when I look at her I feel the burning desire of wishing I could have her breasts. Feeling less than another is fucking toxic, and yet we indulge it. It's what eats us inside to point we take our own lives. To try to stack rank ourselves to the cis feminine beauty standard is destructive behavior and I don't know how to change that or even if it's okay to ask that we should try, but it's harmful thinking. Extremely so.

19 March 2016
Queering straight
Some nights like these I feel like a fraud. A pretend girl, a pretend queer, a pretend lesbian. That I'm really straight because I have a different package down below and I like girls and I operated in boymode for so long. But tonight while taking a shower feeling desperate about my body, realizing that no matter how hard I try to fulfill the desire my body so anxiously reminds of every minute the day, the constant klaxon going off asking me "why does this body have these parts?" And intruding into my internal dialog with "These are not the right parts" "These feelings and nerves are alien to us" "These parts are not the the correct body style for the underlying chassis please correct this"; I realized that while I might never know peace with the physical sex of my body, this body has been more stilled than before. That this body, though conflicted, is claiming a space reserved for cisgender women, and that the mere act of having *this* body style and having changed my name and my pronouns and having given my body life preserving medication that gives me some small sense of peace is *queer as fuck*. That yes I have a girlfriend and yes our naked bodies may resemble a straight heteronormative

relationship as a snapshot in time but how we live and experience our lives is the queerest thing in the world because we take what would look straight and queer the fuck
out of it to the point that nobody can draw clean lines
anymore between who can be gay and who can be straight and
that when we queer straightness, we tear down every bound-
ary and label that is holding everyone back. That we are
reclaiming the colonized world of heteronormativity AND
homonormativity and re-wilding it back to a state where
bodies can just be bodies and people can heal themselves
and love each other without fearing who is gay or who is
straight. Trans men and women are queering gay and queering straight and with that thought I realized I am "queer
enough" I am "woman enough" I am "gay enough" and that
persistent alarm inside my body, that constant intrusive
voice was made quieter by the booming voice of this reali-
zation that resonated through my body and opened my bones
and my meat and my pores and this wild and wonderful crea-
ture of a woman rose like wind from deep inside and planted
herself in this body, ready to blossom and grow like a wild
jungle over the world, ready tear apart the broken systems
like weeds from growing a crack. You can kill us but you
can't kill us all and we will not stop until everything is
queer and wild and wonderful and free.

Sunday, March 20, 2016 at 7:41am CDT
Rule 39 in the comedian's handbook: Trans women are always good for a cheap laugh.

Thursday, March 24, 2016 at 3:41am CDT
What happened in NC yesterday is only a harbinger of what's yet to come. It started in Houston and it will roll over trans women across this country like a steamroller.

Wednesday, April 6, 2016 at 9:50am CDT
I'm closing up facebook media shop.

I posted to Facebook asking if found hair ties were fair game. A man replied to my post saying there were cases of people contracting MRSA from using found hair ties. I felt REALLY embarrassed and deleted the post, leaving a comment just before I deleted the post letting the man know "hey I feel really embarrassed about asking this question, I'm gonna delete this post now and thank you so much for the heads up".

He then sent me the following messages on Facebook Messenger, thinking I had blocked him. I subsequently deleted my Facebook account and I am no longer actively participating on Facebook anymore.

Next Page: Trigger Warning.

David Brown   9:04am

wtf you stupid twat, blocking me for warning you against the genuine risk of infection from filthy hair ties? GET MRSA and get your limbs cut off and die in a hot mess of gangene you piece of crap, scumbag!

David Brown   9:18am

blocked me for warning her that her habit of using hair ties found in parking lots can lead to health consequences, ie documented cases of MRSA infection from dirty hair ties. I was blocked so fast I did not even see the parting 'fuck you' message. The topic has been heavily researched by the females of my household. This is what I get for being FUCKING HELPFUL!
LikeShow more reactionsCommentShare
1Roman Gaidier
Comments
Arkin Tidrick
Arkin Tidrick I sincerely hope the wretch dies in a hot mess of gangrene! INGRATE!

David Brown   9:32am

YOU CAN NOT MANSPLAIN TO A FUCKING MAN IN A DRESS!

David Brown

Women" in Tech (self.GenderCritical)

submitted 1 day ago by introveritas

A male programmer friend recently attended a women's tech event. "I bet there were a lot of straight men there," I said. "Oh no, I was only one of 3 men invited. It was a WOMEN'S event." After I asked more about it, and he admitted about a quarter of the attendees were transwomen. "That's what I meant!" I said. He said that the leader of the event was a transwoman. "She really was comfortable asserting authority!" In fact, the more he thought about it, the more he realized transwomen were "leading" the women's events, while the women tended to be a lot quieter and draw less attention to themselves. In our long conversation, he mentioned a tech organization that had created a position for a woman, and received mostly applications from transwomen. The woman doing the hiring was put in the difficult position of having to define "woman" for the sake of the applicants, and not wanting to create a shitstorm she surrendered: "fine, anyone who defines themselves as a woman." He said at most general tech events, almost all of the "women" attending are transwomen.

Women are drastically underrepresented in tech. The MtT's in tech are undermining every effort to increase women's participation and probably driving women away even more. All while femmewashing their enterprises, because if they say they're women in tech, then there's no sexism any more.

Dimming Toward a Darker Age

9 April 2016

Sunday, March 20, 2016 at 6:33am

Yesterday I stumbled across Joppa, founded in 1872 by slaves freed in Dallas by the emancipation proclamation. It is one of the last remaining freedman's towns still in existence. The settlement is wedged between the trinity river, a freeway and an unforgiving rail line, difficult to access and uninviting to the outside. "Inside" is a town where the southern blackness of freed slaves has been allowed to mind its own damn business for almost 150 years, free from the ever encroaching march of "Dallas Progress" that tears down and erases history in favor of erecting facades of southern music, art, flavors, and religion while pushing the authentic voices off the land and into oblivion, AKA "further south". I drove through not even really understanding what the place was at the time, I was a wayward queer white girl lost in south Dallas, but I understood enough to know that I should at the very least carry love and respect in my heart as I searched for the road out. I found one of the three unmarked roads out under an imposing freeway, and looking in my rearview mirror as I passed under the overpass, I saw churches and shotgun houses and horses and muddy banks and chickens, a town bordered by train tracks, bayou and freeways, shaded by rust, textured by peeling paint and tinted by minty marshland grasses. I bid farewell and pulled out onto the freeway. Milo looked at me and asked me what the place was and I decided it was time to explain to him what whiteness and blackness are, how our histories violently came together and violently diverged, how that violence cleaved south Dallas from north Dallas and how government policies create multi- generational classes that are divided by race, with white landowners still the winners and freed black women and men still working to raise their children against this tide, and how the land we were driving through is land that the people in this area have worked hard to keep, and if anything, that ought to be respected and not something white people think we can just own, that no, this is black culture in this place, that yes we are all one race under the colors of our skin, but how we live and who we are is not something that can be bought and sold on a commercial market defined by the white man's rule, that how we all live should be held in our hearts as good and true and sometimes we should just know when to leave well enough alone without our ideas of what a place could be or should be, and instead just let a place be. And by that point we were in Pleasant Grove, on a bearing towards Casa View where I was raised. I realized as we approached the intersection at Gus Thomason and Ferguson roads that I am, at my core, a southern reformation Protestant girl, that I can't ever deny that no matter how worldly an air I may try to put on to cover that up; that my business ain't in Joppa and their business has the right to remain their own business if that's how they prefer it, that blackness is their blackness and is not here to serve me knowing my whiteness, but I already let it and in that moment of momentary regret, because I had stolen from the black people as a way of understanding more completely my whiteness, said a prayer for that place I had seen and asked the God I was raised with to forgive me for stealing their voice to know my own and to help me love better the city that gave me who I am while I waited for the arrow to give me a sign.

10 April 2016

When I was a teenager I had two boyfriends. Though at the time I wouldn't dared to have cast those friendships as such, they were my boyfriends. My first boyfriend had a motorcycle. At 13 and 14 years old I would sneak out, he would pick me up on his motorcycle and we would go to punk clubs in Dallas. I would ride on the back and hold tight around his waist as he took me all over Dallas. Once I spent an entire summer there at his place and we'd ride that motorcycle everywhere. He had girlfriends and they would come over and make out and have sex and sleep over with him while I slept on a bean bag couch. I was jealous but he didn't know I wanted him to be my boyfriend and I really didn't understand that I wanted to be his girl-friend either. But he protected me and took care of me and looked after me and it was love for whatever the type of teenage love it was that we could have in Dallas in 1988, with me a closeted a trans girl and him a tough punk who rode motorcycles. I don't know where he is now and I'm sure if I told him all this he would probably murder me on the spot no joke. I'm happy knowing now that what we had was love, it was the kind of sweet teenage love a boy and a girl can share. I know this in my heart now so even though at the time I didn't know what all this meant, perhaps it was better this way because what I did get to have was pretty goddamn sweet. I'll talk about the other boyfriend some other time.

11 April 2016

I am mad at my waist. GIRL UP YOU FUCKING MAN TORSO.

13 April 2016

Me: "I've just...always had a difficult time initiating sex."
(launches into a complex litany of possible reasons why because trans, my body and dysphoria)
GF: "maybe it's because you're a girl and girls are taught we're not supposed to do that"
Me:(blink blink)
GF: "baby, you're a girl. You always have been.

17 April 2016

I wish I could explain to cis people what it feels like to have a nationwide political party put into their platform a set of policies that will literally eliminate your ex-istence. It's like…they are against abortion except when they want to abort trans women from the United States. It's more than controlling access to my body, it's about controlling my right to exist. I can't think of a single worse set of policies put forth by a political party. It's fucking horrifying and I like, don't wanna believe it, but the Republican Party platform is create a world so hostile to trans women that we simply never are allowed to exist in public. I wish I could make cis people feel what it's like to have your identity in total to be denied from existence, and instead be forced to live an identity that's not yours. It's…devastating. I wish I could convey this feeling.

17 April 2016
Trans parenting
Is lying in bed crying on a rainy Sunday afternoon, thinking about all the years I was irritated and angry, trying to understand why everything felt so wrong for all those years I was trying to "be the dad" according to the binary gender norms and utterly failing. Remembering All the ways I failed my children and how now they are almost all grown and I'm watching my eleven year old son slip into growing up and his childhood beginning to slowly recede. What I would do to be able to go back to be their mom, instead of the confused, irritated, angry asshole I was. I carry a lot regrets. One the one hand I'm glad I get a chance to live the second half of my life better than I did the first half, but damn there are moments where the weight of those lost decades push through and all I can do is lay down in private and cry and hope my children weren't too harmed by the terrible ways I used to behave.

21 April 2016
In 9 days Tina and I get keys to our place. Two years ago today I was homeless. This has been the hardest fucking three years of my life but I will prevail.

2016-05-05 08:54:10.793

People do not understand that when trans women begin to be erased from the daylight, it is the signal that our civilization is slowly dimming toward a darker age.

When we, trans women, emerge into the light, we mark the promise a better possible world. When we emerge and are allowed to exist in public is when you may allow yourself to know the world is healing and getting better.

When trans women are no longer actively protected and forced back into the shadows is when everyone else who does not "fit the mold" should look behind their shoulders and wonder if that dark force that erased trans women is now hunting for them.

2016-05-10 08:17:35.443
WE SEE YOU

I'll probably start crying after I calm down from my fist-pumping joy that the DOJ just fully, completely, with no ambiguous words, addressed the struggles of transgender people and gave us validity. Holy freaking goddamn shit.

2016-05-25 12:35:21.96
Just so people know. The state of Texas and 10 other states sued the DOJ. The State of Texas is suing on behalf of Harrold ISD which on Monday night passed a policy that denies trans children the right to use facilities that matches their gender and sex, which is a policy that eliminates trans people from our country by never allowing a trans child to fully develop. Biological Essentialism followed to its logical end looks like this. I carry in my heart a lot of pain every day. Listening to Ken Paxton a few minutes ago announce this lawsuit fills me with a rage and grief that I am unable to carry safely.

This shit has GOT to fucking stop people.

2016-06-07 13:44:15.397
What cis people feel when first confronted with the bathroom question I *think* feels very similar to how I as a trans person felt when I was first confronted with no longer able to use the men's room (because let me tell you, the stares were getting really bad). The feeling is one

of anxiety and panic, the world feeling like it's turning upside down, the fear is real. It is scary to confront our societies rules around "where girls and boys are allowed".

I understand that fear. I don't want ANYONE to have to feel it. Cis, Trans, whoever.

Cis people fear: "If I can't reliably tell men from women then how to we enforce gender segregation and keep women safe from men seeking to harm?"
Trans people fear: "I need to use the bathroom where I feel the safest and I can't reliably tell which restroom that is."

So how do we alleviate these fears for *everyone*?

Well, we need to break it down a little.

The fear we *all* feel is abstracted to: "I can't reliably tell x from y anymore, I just want to feel safe".

That means both cis AND trans are experiencing a very similar feeling around the bathrooms, a fear that I would say is transnormative, because for trans people that fear goes WAY WAY WAY beyond just the freaking damn restroom. Trans people feel that *EVERYWHERE*. Because that fear of the gendered and sexed world breaking down is baked into the trans experience, it is IMO a large part of what makes "the trans experience". Ergo, bathroom panic is a transnormative experience that cis people are having to confront and feel. So cis people who have "the bathroom fear", welcome to trans personhood.

So what the in the ever loving fuck do we do about this?

My preference is that *NO ONE* feels bathroom fear. I don't want cis people to have to live with the bathroom fear and I don't want trans people to have to worry about cis people who have the bathroom fear acting rudely or violently towards trans people just trying to get by in the world.

I believe the best way to accomplish this is for cis people to stop thinking about "what if I can't tell x from y anymore" and just go back to the firmer ground of cis personhood. Trans people will probably never feel all that secure navigating sex and gender in the world because the biological dominance of the cis majority, so I feel that if cis people remain on firm ground at least the transnormative panic and anxiety is not magnifying in the world.

So why do cis people need to stop being afraid then?

Here's the deal: Cisnormativity is a *HUGE MASSIVE* force, like, cis people, you can't even begin to realize just how much force and power cisnormativity exerts on *literally everything we do as a species*. That's why a single issue where the gendered and sexed rules go into liminiality can cause what looks like to me an almost segregationist split in this country. Cisnormativity demands SO FUCKING MUCH. Trust me please, it's like a crushing atmosphere you can't escape when your gender "slips out" of cisnormativity.

Since cisnormativity is such a huge overwhelming force, NO ONE is going to go traipse through transnormativity for the larfs. There's a reason why gender nonconforming (trans incl.) people worry so much and struggle about all this, because it's not just some random ass thing you up and decide one day. Cisnormativity DOMINATES. Cis people, the gender construct you live in *crushes* gender NC ppl. Literally no one is going to just one day decide to be one gender and the next day decide to be another. Cisnormativity will never allow that.

So basically that means cis people, you can just forget about the bathroom thing and go back into cisnormativity. You can literally stop worrying about it. Cisnormativity protects you.

Once you all stop worrying about it, trans people can have one less thing to worry about as well! And one basic part of our overall life anxiety "because trans" is lessened because now the anxiety of "which bathroom best suits my gender" does not have the additional fear of worrying about wether or not cis people are having a similar gender liminal freakout.

So to wrap it all up: cis people, get out of my trans experience and go back to being cis.

2016-06-10: (slack chat at work)
My biggest concern over the next 18 months is all this crap going around about trans people leading to escalated violence against trans people who already experience much greater levels of harassment and violence than the non-trans portion of the population. In the past three months the amount of shit I catch from people has been increasing because the GOP is tacitly saying "these people are per-verted rapists". I would really like that shit to stop.

Pulse

2016-06-12 11:16:31.407

Make no mistake this was a terrorist attack directly aimed at LGBT people.

My heart pours out to Muslim queer people who inevtably will be erased by the coming onslaught of islamaphobia.

My heart has been ripped out.

I knew it was gonna get fucked up going into the election season but this is just devastating.

And can everyone please center on LGBT people

My wife is 2300 hundred miles away and it'll be weeks before I can hold her. I just can't deal right now.

The vigil and march in downtown Austin tonight feels like a galvanizing moment here. I hope this feeling does not fade, that our memories remain long and our defiant ferocity compels us all to fight for equality to our last breath.

2016-06-30 17:26:06.257

Trans people getting better treatment and acceptance shouldn't have to bear the burden of solving all the evils of colonization and patriarchy in the process. Like, my right to my existence on my terms owes neither the patriarchy nor the human rights activists or anyone's political agenda for that matter.

To Our Last Breath

2016-07-15 16:01:29.43
y'all I'm kinda tired of having to bear witness to my suffering in order to expand other people's worldviews.

20 July 2016

I think how we all view gender is dependent on how we each perceive the competing maps of what a body is and how a gender lives in it. The lines of battle have been established at the disputed borders of all these maps and have been laid over trans people as proof that a particular map is more accurate or better. I think this is extremely unfair to trans people who don't feel like their body should be defined by someone else'e map, yet there are considerable numbers of groups of trans and cis people who feel like this is a perfectly reasonable burden to place on the entire trans community.

"I'm trans" because I am that way. My reasons as to why do not need to make sense to myself or anyone else, nor do they have to fit into any ideas of what gender is historically or what it's supposed to be. There are so many oppositional groups (trans to cis, leftist to conservative) drawing maps over my body and trying to determine for me exactly how I get to exist along their ideology. I get very upset with this because I feel like I do not actually have agency no matter where I go. I always have to conform with whatever ideological territory that has been mapped over me in a particular space without my consent. I say I "have to" because when I don't, the social constructs begin falling apart in unpredictable ways and I find myself in one or even up to dozens of a hundred different ideological conflicts that I wish to be no part of. I just want to be me. Not evidence, not a data point, just me.

2016-08-09 13:10:05.51

I live in a broken space in my head that I've done well enough to mask, hide, cope and manage with my whole life. About 4 months ago I decided that I was done trying to pretend like I'm not broken, and now I just get real with people and do my best to reassure them that I'm not some fragile case of about to lose my shit and freak out, but instead that I have made a pretty useful and functional life out of a some pretty tough circumstances in my head, that I'm tired of pretending like I'm okay and I need someplace in my life where I can just be completely fucked up and broken and accepted as I am and allowed to just be a complete and total fucking unregulated mess - Because white-knuckling through this all the time has ground me down to the point where most days the every-minute struggle I go through to function no longer seems worth the price of living.

2016-08-27 10:31:17.483

I think even though religion is part of the anti-trans legal phalanx being attempted in the US, it is important to understand how the message they use to peddle anti-trans woman fears has a broad and devastating reach that extends well beyond the ideological boundaries of Christian GOP supporters.

The message of fear and the social buttons they are managing to push with this issue are, from a Machiavellian perspective, incredibly good politics because it rallies far and wide across race, gender, class and religion. They have made trans women their "La raison de l'autre" in a couple of ways, by othering trans women into pedophiles and perverts, by also setting a distinction for themselves as the "other option" that seeks to shows the republican party as the party of reason that stands against all this madness.

By moving the focus off the "bathroom" issue and showing this to be part of a broader campaign to effectively erase a group of people from the U.S and force us back into "cis compliance", we reframe the issues in a new light that centers the focus on how these efforts *feel* to trans people. We take the focus off cis people fearing trans women and turn that into compassion for ALL trans people.

Epilogue›

14 September 2016
For trans women just starting to confront the gender question for themselves:
Your relationship to your body is more important than your relationship to social gender IMO. I believe that when you "get right" with your body the rest will follow suit.

Ask yourself "Do you want estrogen in your body? Do you want breasts? Do you want smooth skin? Do you want smooth curves?"

If so, give yourself that gift. Changing your name, gender marker, yadda yadda, you can decide that later.

If you are experiencing anxiety and panic, and are concerned about starting HRT, I want to you to know that in my case, part of what causes my severe anxiety and panic *IS* the testosterone in my body. When it goes up, I literally feel the waves of anxiety and panic flitting at the horizons of my perception and as T rises, it comes over me like a hurricane. So getting the T out of your system my help you too.

If you feel like transition means you'll just end up acting out another role, if you are wondering what the hell gender even is, or if you even care about having one or not, I get that. It took me a long time to get to the point where I could just accept myself as the woman I am, to where I could even imagine that I deserved a body. I wasn't able to comfortably feel that for the first…sheesh almost 3 years. It's only been really recently that I even feel like having *any* name or relationship to my body is no longer this foreign, alien concept. I understand now what "feeling grounded" means.

Basically, you're not "transitioning" you are *aligning*. And whatever that means to you, that's your truth. There's no right or wrong way to align yourself.

This is your life, your body, your process. This is not

a race to a finish line. I do believe though, if you suffer anxiety and have a desire for an estrogen body, that you should seriously consider starting HRT and committing yourself at least 4-8 weeks on HRT to see if HRT is something that will work for you. In my experience going from "I want HRT" to a doctor telling me "your prescription is ready" took 5 months. When I got my first rx (I actually didn't get the meds and waited another year to start) my intent was to do the "take it for 8 weeks and see" but my wife at the time FREAKED and I decided not to do it and wait. By the following year I was at the point where I was either going to kill myself or commit to HRT. So I would recommend doing the "8 week test" ASAP and NOT waiting until you're "Certain what you wanna do". The "wait until you're certain" path is NOT harm reduction.

You know the status quo is not working. You have to step off this square. You begin getting off this square by doing the smallest possible tests you can so you can begin to see what works for you.

Whether you realize it yet or not, you are already an explorer and well on your way. You have already "slipped out" and started your adventure. Welcome to the light, I am a helper.

www.ingramcontent.com/pod-product-compliance
Lightning Source LLC
Chambersburg PA
CBHW050456290526
45786CB00006B/2313